basketry

Basic Techniques **Explained**
Step by **Step**

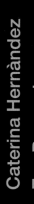

Caterina Hernàndez
Eva Pascual

Schiffer Publishing Ltd

4880 Lower Valley Road • Atglen, PA 19310

© 2013 Schiffer Publishing, Ltd.
Library of Congress Control Number: 2013953534

ISBN: 978-0-7643-4471-8
Printed in The United States of America

Published by Schiffer Publishing, Ltd.
4880 Lower Valley Road
Atglen, PA 19310
Phone: (610) 593-1777; Fax: (610) 593-2002
E-mail: Info@schifferbooks.com

For the largest selection of fine reference books
on this and related subjects, please visit our
website at **www.schifferbooks.com.**
You may also write for a free catalog.

This book may be purchased from the publisher.
Please try your bookstore first.

We are always looking for people to write books
on new and related subjects. If you have an idea
for a book, please contact us at
proposals@schifferbooks.com.

Schiffer Books are available at special discounts for bulk
purchases for sales promotions or premiums. Special
editions, including personalized covers, corporate imprints,
and excerpts can be created in large quantities for special
needs. For more information contact the publisher.

Originally released in Spanish as *Cestería*.
Copyright © 2006 by Parramón Ediciones, S.A.
Translated by Omicron Language Solutions
Photographs: Nos & Soto
Layout and page make-up: Estudi Guasch, S.L.

Other Schiffer Books on Related Subjects:

basketry

Materials and tools

Basic techniques

Step by step

presen

Today's basketry is the modern awakening of a dream that has been with us since the very beginning of mankind and still has the shadowy, but more than dignified, occupation of providing us with useful objects. Across the centuries, the work of all of history's anonymous basket makers have been making tiny contributions to the craft, so that today, one piece represents a compendium of all their experiences: the finest plant material the earth has to offer, the best way to weave it, and the perfect shape to make it useful to us in our day-to-day activities.

All of this, however, is being brought into question and threatened by our modern way of life; time has new value and markets are nonsensical. A deeper knowledge and a fresh look at basketry could bring about a rediscovery of these useful objects and a greater appreciation of their many authentic values: aesthetic

tation

and economic; historic and environmental; intellectual and human. A piece of basketry is a hot object.

In the tools and materials section, we will take a look at the relationship between basketry and natural resources provided by nature; in this case, the native plants of the authors' country of origin. We will explain how to find and prepare different materials and describe some techniques for weaving pieces of basketry. In the step-by-step guides we will show several basket makers making a selection of objects as a guide for those who would like to replicate them or just get to know a bit more about them. In the image gallery, which can be found towards the end of this book, we will briefly show you how to work with the materials and apply the techniques used by modern basket makers.

There are a great many materials that can be woven together to make baskets. Here, a selection of local materials is shown that is representative of the main types of vegetation used. Readers can incorporate the plant life in their local environment to suit their needs, in the best tradition of basket makers.

In terms of the tools needed, a knife is essential, but there are some tools shown here that can make basketry easier and give better results.

Materials and tools

MATERIALS

Willow and Serge

Some trees and shrubs, especially if they have been pruned, sprout a few rods of variable length and thickness every year. They are woody but flexible enough to work with.

On a winter walk, anyone can collect rods of different species: hazel, wild rose, olive, elm, birch, or ash, among others.

Any branch without subdivisions can be used green if it is long enough to wrap a couple of times around your hand (between knuckles and thumb) without breaking.

Wood is good for making rigid, strong basketry; it can be rough or smooth and can be worked with its bark intact or peeled.

Some of the best plants to work with are the *salicaea* known as willow and serge. These are amongst the most popular materials used in basketry for many reasons; the long, fine stems are flexible, yet rigid once woven. They come in many different shapes, sizes, colors, and varieties. There is also a long tradition of their use and our knowledge of them.

There are more than three hundred varieties of Salix, osier, or willow, such as *Salix Viminalis, Salix Alba, Salix Purpurea* and *Salix Caprea*. These share some characteristics but are not identical in terms of flexibility, color, texture, preferred climate, etc.

They grow near rivers and other places where there is water, which is willow's only non-negotiable demand. Wild shrubby types, such as *Salix Purpurea, Salix Caprea*, etc., are known as serge and can be found alongside water

Willow in summer.

Willow in winter.

Bundles of willow and serge.

Piece woven with three colors of willow and serge.

BLACK WILLOW

courses. Willow for weaving also comes from basket willows, which are especially cultivated for the purpose; mostly *Salix Alba* and *Salix Viminalis* but other varieties are also used.

This is a deciduous tree or shrub with lanceolate leaves, which is often radically pruned to a few centimeters above ground level to obtain the greatest possible number of long stems.
This willow, when used with the bark intact, offers hues of green, grey, black, brown, red or yellow. It is cut in winter and can be used immediately, although this can result in a less firm basket as willow contracts when dry. It is better to dry it then soak it before use. This is done by submerging a bundle of stems in a container of water, such as an old

bath or large basin. Soaking times vary: one week in summer and two in winter, although soaking time can reduced by using hot water. Do not exceed soaking time as the bark will come off and the stem will become brittle. After soaking, take the bundle out of the water and keep it wrapped in a plastic sheet or cloth. Soaked black willow retains moisture and can be worked for up to a week after soaking if the climate is not too dry. Note that it cannot be worked once it has dried because a second soaking will cause the bark to come off.

Willow rods.

Willow.

Buff willow tray.

White willow rattle.

White willow
egg basket.

WHITE WICKER

This is stripped willow. It can either be bought ready-stripped or collected in the spring, when the sap is rising, when leaves are beginning to sprout, or just before. To strip the stem, trap the tip between the two parts of a folded branch, then with one hand keep the branch folded, and keeping an even pressure on the stem slide it along, tip to base, through the makeshift peeler with the other hand. The bark will come off completely and the stem can be left to dry and kept until needed. White willow needs a shorter soaking time than black willow: about four hours, depending on the temperature of the water and the thickness of the stems. It is ready to work after soaking but it is best to let it rest for a few hours first, wrapped in a dampened plastic sheet.

Another characteristic of white willow is that it dries more quickly and often has to be re-soaked in the middle of a work session because the tips tend to break. A second soaking does not damage white willow.

BUFF WILLOW

This is another type of barkless wicker on the market. It has a toasted color and is quite shiny: stems are boiled with the bark on, a process that allows some of the bark's color to penetrate, giving the stems their toasted hue. Buff willow only needs two or three hours soaking, plus the same time wrapped, but not submerged.

White and buff willow.

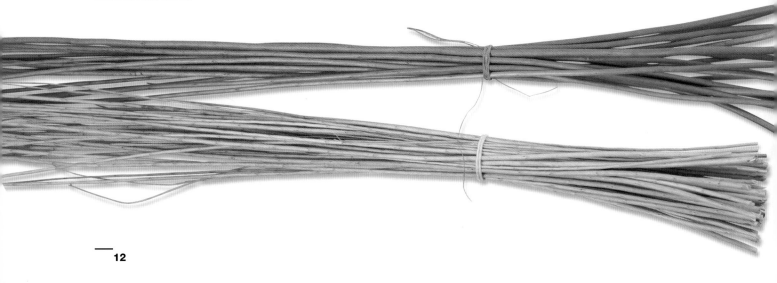

Split in two.

Willow strips and split willow.

SPLIT WILLOW AND STRIPS

Wicker can also be worked in strips. These are available, mechanically produced, in specialist shops. Otherwise, stems can be split into two or three lengthwise.

This way, willow can be used in the same way as wooden strips.

Fairly thick stems are needed for splitting; these need to be recently cut from the willow tree or soaked (they would break if used dry). Cut the tips with secateurs, and then use a knife to make an incision in the finest end, where the split will start. It can be split in two using just your hands and knees:

take the two parts of the stem, one in each hand, trap the willow between your knees; pull the two halves apart and the stem will split into two equal parts from the stem to the base.

The three-way cleave, as the name suggests is a tool used to split a stem into three. After making the initial cut with a knife, the cleave is pushed down through the length of the stem, separating the stem into three as it goes. You can control the regularity of the division by turning the stem and cleave or changing the angle. If a cleave is not available, you can use the tips of your

thumbs, your index finger and middle finger.

The fine, de-barked strip does not take long to soak, and will dry very quickly too.

Split willow with bark soaks and dries quickly, as if it were white willow, but cannot be soaked again as it will lose its skin.

Starting the split with a knife.

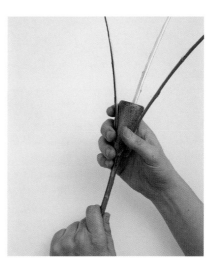

Split into three.

13

Chestnut tree.

Splitting the grain of the wood with an axe.

Chestnut

The woody stems of some trees, prepared as strips, can be worked to produce pieces of basketry. The result is rigid, strong and feels like untreated wood.

The look of the piece will vary greatly depending on the fineness of the strips and whether the bark is included in the work. Chestnut, oak, hazel, mimosa and willow, amongst others, can be worked on this way. Strips of wood can be bought in specialist shops or on the internet. If not, you can prepare it yourself, although this is not an easy task. The chestnut (*Castanea sativa*) is a deciduous tree that grows in

temperate and cool, humid climates, free of drought. For basketry, shoots that appear close to the main trunk and grow long straight and unbranched are usually used. These shoots are prepared as strips after being cut when they reach a diameter of two to six centimeters. They can be prepared and worked immediately in the green, or properly stored for later use. If you are going to store them, keep the thicker stems submerged in water and the thinner ones can be kept dry.

To convert the stored stems into fine, manageable strips, impregnate them with water and heat them in an oven

for several hours; then, with a knife, separate a few layers that follow the grain of the wood and smooth them down by running the strip between your knee and the knife.

The strips can be kept dry for as long as necessary but they will need soaking to restore their flexibility before you can work with them.

Soaking time will vary according to thickness.

Chestnut pannier.

Chestnut basket.

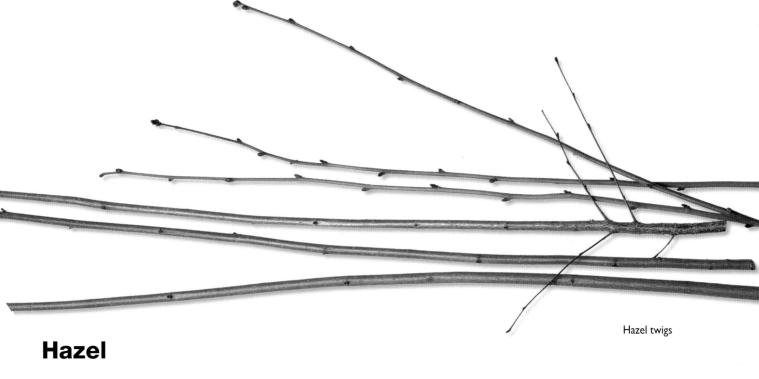

Hazel

The hazel (Corylus avellana) grows in mountain woodland and is cultivated (rain fed or irrigated), for its fruit, the hazelnut. It usually grows as clustered branches, without a distinct trunk. In basketry, the rods are used, mostly in strips. They are not as flexible as willow and so cannot be worked in such a large variety of ways.

It is easy to make hazel strips using just a knife. Choose a straight, unbranched stem of between one and three centimeters thick that is growing directly from the ground. Cut it and while it is still green, make a small cut across the stem halfway along the stem to the depth that you want the thickness of the strip to be. Take the stem with one hand on either side of the cut, support the opposite side with your knee and bend it gently. The curve separates outwards into a strip, starting from the cut, and if you slide it along your knee, the strip will split lengthwise from the stem. Next, smooth it by running it between your knee and your knife.

You can get several strips from each stem, which you can leave to dry and keep until needed, and then soak them before weaving them.

Hazel trees in winter.

Hazel basket.

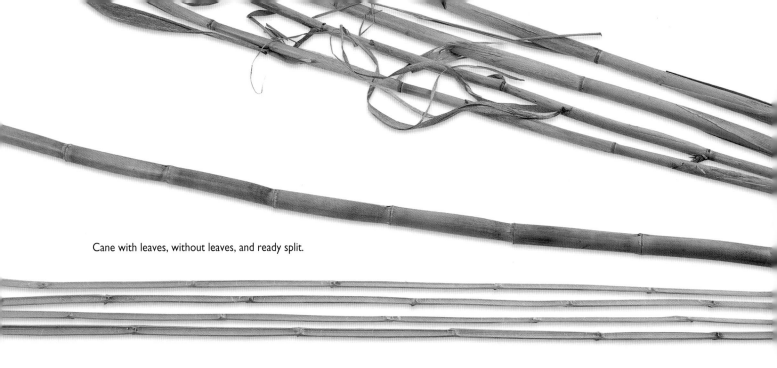

Cane with leaves, without leaves, and ready split.

Cane

The cane (*Arundo donax*) is a huge grass that lives in temperate to warm regions. It is very common in the Mediterranean region.

The stem is woody, very hard, and very light when it is intact and dry, but flexible if split lengthways and slightly damp. It is not one of the most pleasant materials to work with because it is easy to get cuts and very sharp splinters from it, but it grows abundantly and is cheap and easy to find. In its native lands, it has always been widely used in agriculture, construction, basketry and many other

activities, from fishing to music and children's games.

In basketry, it is used alone or combined with willow: in this case the sections of the piece that need to be durable and strong (base, rim and handles), are woven with willow, which is more suitable for the task, while the walls are woven with cane. This method provides a lighter and stronger basket than one made from willow alone. One-year-old unbranched, flowerless stems are chosen, cut at the base in winter and left to dry in the

sun. Once dried, they can be kept as long as necessary. To prepare the cane (we recommend using gloves for this task), remove the leaves that surround the stem (a knife will be sufficient) and divide it lengthwise into strips, with a knife or cleave. The cane cleave is a cylindrical tool that has a sharp edge. After starting off the cut with a knife, the cleave is pushed in between the grain of the cane and splits it lengthways. The cleave is partially enclosed by the outer part to let the already separated strips of cane pass

Cane combined with wicker.

Well reinforced cane weave.

Base woven in cane.

Canes.

through while protecting the hand of the person who is working it (split cane cuts like a razor if you are even slightly careless). By turning the cane and the cleave, you can control the direction of the split. Each node on the cane requires a tap on the cleave.

Once split, cane strips need to be refined with a knife and dampened. Then they can be worked in a perpendicular or circular weave, if you twist the strip to get rid of the cane's stiffness. Cane basketry requires great mastery of the technique, it is not an easy material and is hazardous to work with, but it can make pieces of great beauty that are strong, tough and light. Cane can also be used to give strength and rigidity to the weave of some wicker baskets while adding hardly any weight: when the wall is woven, before making the rim, introduce strips of cane alongside the stakes next to the base.

This process can be used when making cane objects that need added strength.

Splitting cane.

Start of the split.

Harvested wheat.

Field of wheat.

Straw

Traditionally, straw from cereals that have been grown for food is used for basketry. Wheat (*Triticum sativum*), rye (*Cecale cereale*), oats (*Avena sativa*), rice (*Oryza sativa*) or wild grasses that have stiff fragile stems and can be found on a countryside walk can be used. None of these look like they would be good basketry materials but if several stems are used together, this fragility disappears and they gain outstanding flexibility and surprising strength. Straw is more versatile than it seems and the colors and sheen of the stems are rare in the plant kingdom.

Each cereal has its own specific characteristics of color, thickness, strength and flexibility. The more you get to know about them, the more you can exploit these characteristics to produce pieces of basketry.
Straw is cut in summer when the plant is fully grown and the ears are full of grain. It must be handled carefully as it folds easily. If this happens, it cannot be used in a lot of work, especially the finest. It must be cut without processing, or at least without threshing. It should be left to dry in the sun for a few days and kept until it is needed. Then it must

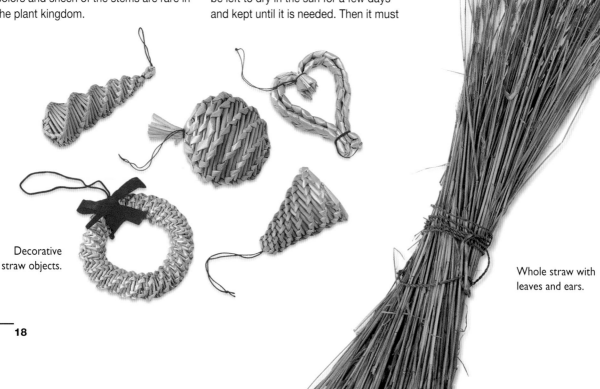

Decorative
straw objects.

Whole straw with
leaves and ears.

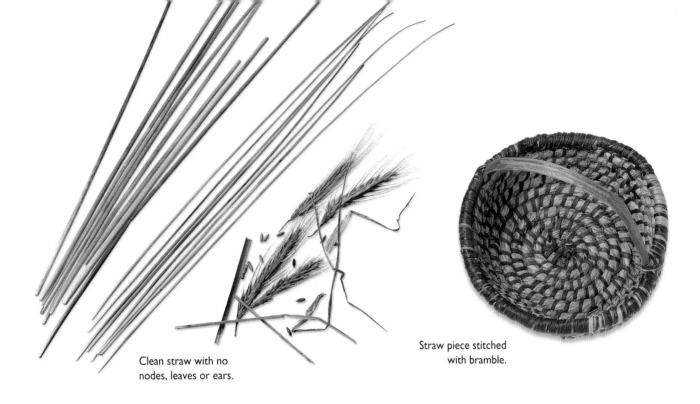

Clean straw with no nodes, leaves or ears.

Straw piece stitched with bramble.

be prepared: separate the ear (if it is not being left on for decorative purposes), trim the nodes and remove the leaves. The useful parts are those that go from node to node. These are classified by size; for more fine work only the part that goes from the ear to the first node is used.

For some pieces, the straw can be split lengthways to achieve a more flexible, flat and smooth material, which can be ironed to make it even flatter.

Before using straw it is important to wet it and leave it for a while for the moisture to soak in. The oldest technique for working straw is known as coiled basketry, sewn with the same or different material such as very fine strips of willow, strips of bramble (*Rubus fructicosus*), esparto grass, and palm leaf, in fact any material that can be rolled and stitched in a coil from the center outwards. Basketry woven using this technique is rigid and surprisingly strong. It can also be worked in a stitched plait, which gives a strong flexible weave, or in the form of ropes or coils, which are more decorative than strong. When split lengthwise, straw can give a colorful, bright weave but it lacks strength so it needs to be glued to cardboard or wood for reinforcement.

Straw crown for carrying loads on the head.

Fine straw piece with red applique.

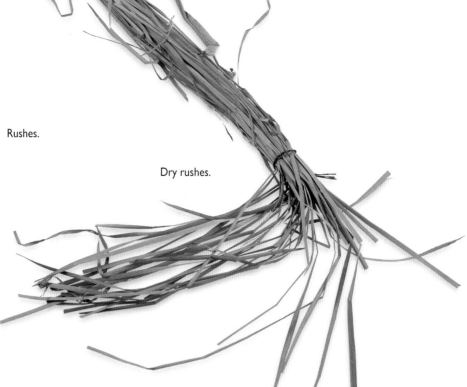

Rushes.

Dry rushes.

Rush

The rush (*Lypna latifolia, Lypna angustifolia)* is a very large grass between one and a half to three meters tall, depending on variety. It grows in quiet waters, boggy areas or on the banks of rivers. The stalk is free of nodes and is wrapped in leaves, which are also long and narrow.

The stems and leaves are thick, soft and spongy. The flower is found at the tip of the stalk and looks like a cigar: long, cylindrical and brown. The plant dies back each year and regrows from the rhizome. It is cut at the end of summer, when it is fully grown and has not yet started to wither. The flowerless plants for cutting are chosen for their height and beauty and are cut from the base with a knife. They are left in the sun to dry, turned now and then protected from

the damp of the night air. Then they are stored.

The plants need to be dampened before working. This can be done by wetting them with a hosepipe and leaving them wrapped in a plastic sheet for a few hours (a day or a night) so that they can absorb the water and are ready to work. Remove the leaves from the plant one by one when you are ready to use them, keeping them wrapped in plastic, damp but not soaked.

Chair seats are often made with rush, this makes them very comfortable and soft thanks to the nature of the plant. It can also be worked as a stitched coil, a stitched plait or as a warp on a more rigid weft.

Child's chair with rush seat.

Rush waste basket.

Detail of a piece of fishing equipment, where the different materials, reed and olive, can be observed.

Reed.

Reed

The reed (*Juncus effusus, Juncus maritimus*, and *Holoschoenus vulgaris*), grows in diverse humid zones, such as mountains, meadows, and marshland. The reed has a large smooth stalk, without nodes; it is strong and flexible with a toast colored flower, whose shape allows us to identify its variety. It is collected in summer, when the plant is healthy and well developed and it is left to dry in the sun. It can then be stored until needed and worked dry if using the tied mesh technique, or damp if using a perpendicular weave or stitched coil techniques.

It is important to check the legislation of each country before collecting reeds as some countries have legislation protecting the wetlands where the reed grows.

The reed has traditionally been used in marine basketry and fishing equipment. It lends great beauty to pieces, along with surprising strength, combined with the transparency of the mesh weave and captivating form.

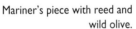

Mariner's piece with reed and wild olive.

Fishing basket made with Catalan coast reed.

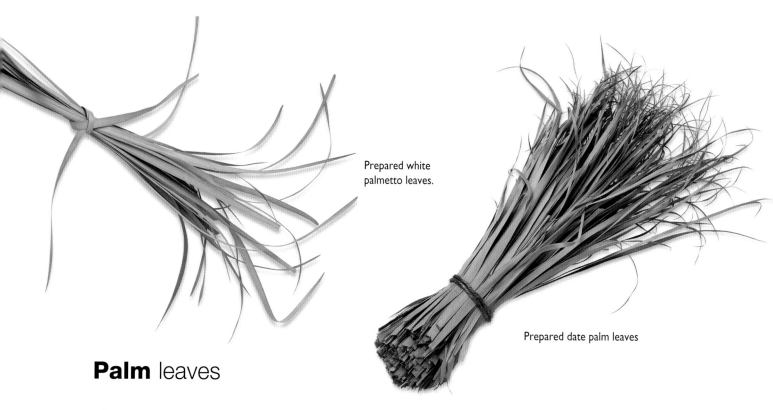

Prepared white palmetto leaves.

Prepared date palm leaves

Palm leaves

Palm trees are perennial and very fibrous. There are many varieties adapted to different climates but they all prefer them to be between temperate and hot. Two examples used in basketry are the date palm and the palmetto.

THE PALMETTO

This is a protected plant in some countries, so check the country's legislation first if you want to collect it. The leaves of the palmetto (*Chamaerops humilis*), with their open hand shape, can be used in two ways:

first, by cutting any open green leaf and leaving it to dry in the sun, then dampening it before use.
This palm is a green, fairly tough material, traditionally used for work items. The second way of using palmetto is removing (without cutting) the unopened leaves; this provides a whiter, softer palm, good for fine basketry. If you are not familiar with the plant or the technique, it is advisable not to do this as it may harm the plant. When dried in the sun, it gets a little whiter, and some people treat it with sulphur to make it even whiter and more flexible.

THE DATE PALM

The green leaf of the date palm (*Phoenix dactylifera*) can be used in a similar way to the green palmetto leaf, although the most outstanding product of this palm tree is white palm. This can only be taken once every four years from each tree, which is bound in winter (as if one was tying an endive so that it grows white inside) so that the leaves grow without any exposure to sunlight. The foliage is separated from the palm leaves, cut at the base and can also be split lengthways (from an incision made with

Palmetto.

Palm.

Stitched palm plait.

Palm basket.

Esparto.

Esparto grass

a nail or needle) to the desired width. It is usually worked in a stitched plait but can also be used to make a stitched coil, perpendicular weave or various types of decorative cords. Palm twists are another outstanding use of this material. Stitched plait pieces are superb for their strength and flexibility.

Esparto (*Stipa tenecissima*) is a very fibrous, strong and flexible grass, which grows in dry, hot and very sunny areas. It can be collected at any time of the year, except in spring, by harvesting entire stalks. This is usually done by wrapping a bundle around a stick and then removing it from the stick. This method lessens the chance of the esparto breaking and it also protects the person picking it from getting cut. After collection, the esparto is left to dry in the sun, then it is

stored and can be dampened just before working. It can be worked in a very fine stitched coil: perpendicular or circular weave, in a stitched plait, a continuous braid, etc.

Esparto is a good all-round material for basketry: robust and strong when needed, and fine and delicate when required.

It can also be crushed or chopped, a process that completely changes its look and texture.

Esparto fireplace fan, with chopped esparto embellishment.

Esparto.

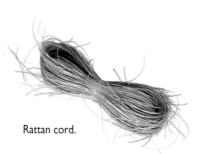

Rattan cord.

Rattan strip.

Chair with rattan strip seat.

Rattan

Rattan (Calamus rotang and other species) is an extraordinary basketry material. It comes from various species of tropical plants with characteristics in common with the palm and vine. It grows very quickly, has very long stems of up to 90 meters in some examples and its uniform thickness means that the basket maker can do away with splices and changes in thickness. Rattan, as well as materials that are extracted from rattan, such as cord and strips, which can be mechanically produced, is mostly seen in basketry imported from tropical countries in Asia and Africa, where it is grown.

MEDULLA

Different thicknesses of medulla are available from craft shops. It is a long smooth strip without nodes, which is very absorbent and flexible when soaked (a very quick process compared to willow). This makes it very easy to work and is even suitable for children to use. It can be used to make a large variety of shapes, for various stitches, and is easy to dye. Its possibilities are endless. Once woven and dry, it is more flexible than willow, so it is often reinforced with a stiffer material.

RATTAN STRIP

This is obtained from the bark of the vine.
Very flexible and strong, it is used for stitching and in various weaves, especially in chair seats with a weave in two or four directions.

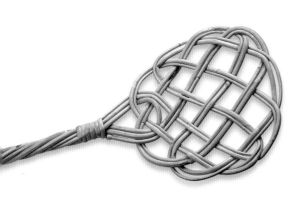

Rattan mattress beater.

Rattan cord pieces.

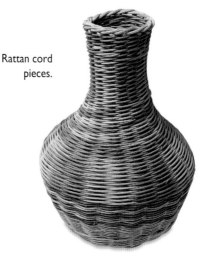

Bamboo quail basket.

Bamboo.

Bamboo

Other materials

In some places, local plants provide materials that offer spectacular properties for basketry, such as bamboo. This is a material with immense potential, but in particular as basketry material when prepared in very fine strips. These are very rigid when woven, so the complete pieces are compact, very strong and incredibly detailed.

Basketry is the craft of making objects using locally available plants. Although basketry materials can be bought, they can also be obtained by getting to know plants and exploring with the goal of discovering original materials. Leaves, shoots, trunks, roots, algae or grasses for weaving can be found everywhere. The plants that have prevailed in each country as basketry materials are probably the ones that give the best results: they are the best to work with; they keep better once worked and

dried or they lend the complete piece a combination of flexibility and rigidity or ventilation and sealing, perfect for specific uses. They are the most beautiful, the easiest to find or cultivate, or they may be the only ones that will grow in some lands with poorer climates. Even so, they are not the only ones that will work.

Piece made with materials gathered on an excursion, including bramble, pine and even sheep wool.

Good basket making materials can be found on a countryside walk.

Curved knives.

Knife.

Secateurs.

Scissors.

TOOLS

FOR CUTTING

Knives: the basket maker's knife cuts and splits all materials, it chops, sharpens, evens, prepares, levers, separates, splices, smooths... It is the principal tool and the only truly indispensable one. The most important thing about knives for basketry work is that they must be strong and always sharp. Because of this they are usually made of iron, which can be sharpened anywhere by hand.

A normal knife can be used for everything, but for certain types of work, basket makers usually use a curved knife. Because it is such a fundamental tool, it is not unusual for the basket maker to entrust his or her special knives to a blacksmith and to have spares available.

Secateurs: these are used for cutting woody materials. Long handled loppers are better for thick branches and secateurs for thinner ones. Secateurs are also used for preparing useful pieces during work and for trimming ends in the complete object and leaving it well finished. This is why they need to be precise and well-sharpened.

Scissors: a simple pair of scissors is all that is needed to cut soft materials, such as straw or palm leaves. They are used in the preparation and the finishing stages.

Craft knife: this tool can be used in the same way as a knife for precise cutting in fine work.

Sharpening stone: this is an indispensable accessory for cutting tools to keep them in prime condition.

Loppers.

Craft knife.

Sharpening stone.

Thick bodkin.

Awl.

Fine bodkin.

Needles.

FOR PUNCTURING, INSERTING, SEWING, SEPARATING

Bodkins: fine and thick bodkins are used according to need. The task of the bodkin isn't so much to puncture the material as to make a space between fibers, where another fiber can be inserted, without breakage. They are finer at the tip so that they can open up a passage between the fibers and as the bodkin gets thicker it widens the gap.

Needles: these are used to stich coils and plaits or to attach different parts of a piece together.

They are thick, long and relatively narrow; they are not very sharp, so that they can pass between the spaces left by the weave without damaging the fibers. The needle is big enough to be able to thread the sewing material.

Awl: this type of awl is a specific tool for working with willow; it is used to open up a gap in the weave to insert a small bundle of tips into the rims and finishes of the piece. Being made of iron, it can also be used to tap the weave, to straighten it, splice it and perfect it. It's useful to have one if you work with willow but you will have to get a blacksmith to make you one as they are not available in the shops.

Pliers: pliers are useful if you need to forcefully pull a fiber that is difficult to move.

Wooden lever: used for making rush seats, to manipulate the material that is to be worked (rush is soft and fragile) without harming it. It is a simple stick of hard wood, sharpened at one end to give it a shape of a rounded screwdriver.

Gimlet: One of the possible ways to finish the opening of baskets made from wooden strips is to pierce the wood using a gimlet and stitch it.

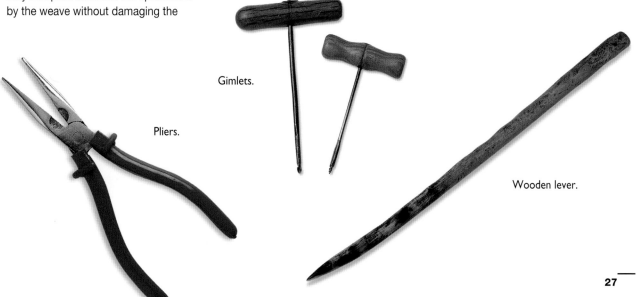

Gimlets.

Pliers.

Wooden lever.

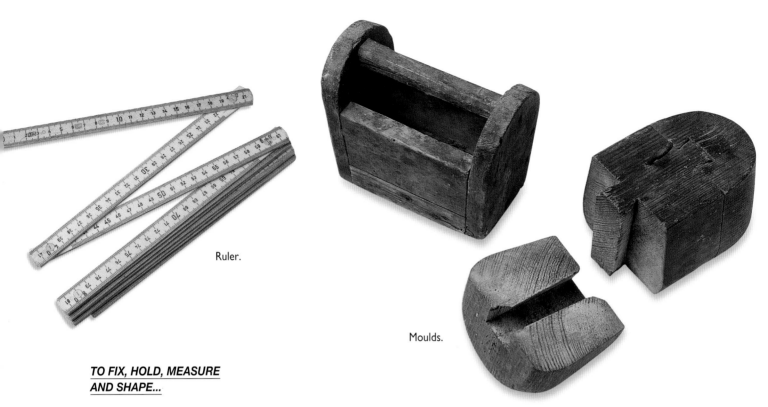

Ruler.

Moulds.

TO FIX, HOLD, MEASURE AND SHAPE...

Rule:r preferably a rigid carpenter's one, a ruler is useful for basket making. For this purpose a rod cut to size for each piece is sometimes used.

Moulds: to achieve a determined shape or a very precise size, moulds are sometimes used. Any object can be a mould: a ball, a box, a can, split wood, pieces of wood attached together or a specially made mould. In the illustrations you can see two wooden moulds for making very small willow pieces; one of them can be taken apart so that it can be removed from the inside of the finished piece.

Clothes pegs: when stems cannot be cut because they are going to be worked back into the piece at a later point, clothes pegs are very useful to temporarily hold them in place or to keep the materials not currently being worked outside of the work space. This can also be done by holding them between your teeth or knees, with cord, or other makeshift accessories.

Wooden mallet: basketry materials aren't malleable. Often they have to be tapped to coerce them into the required position to achieve the shapes we want with the perfection we desire. A wooden mallet allows us to tap materials with minimum damage.

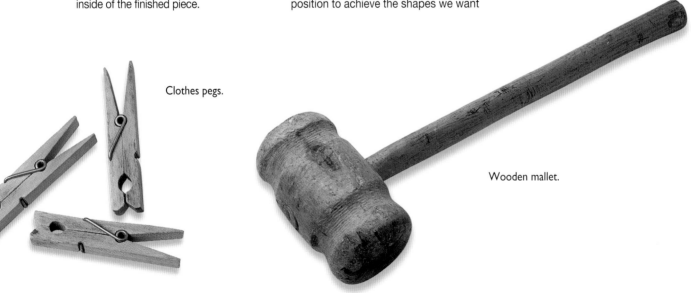

Clothes pegs.

Wooden mallet.

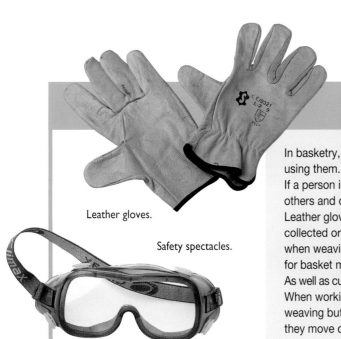

Leather gloves.

Safety spectacles.

Protective gloves and safety spectacles.

In basketry, the tools and materials that are used can be harmful to those using them. Risk awareness is the best prevention.

If a person is not working alone, it is essential to maintain a safe distance from others and discourage visitors.

Leather gloves will protect the hands from the material when it is being collected or when cane is being prepared but it is not advisable to wear gloves when weaving as you lose sensitivity and manual dexterity, which are essential for basket making. You must always work carefully.

As well as cuts and punctures, another typical basket maker's accident is eye injury. When working with long rods or branches, your attention is centerd on weaving but you also need to be aware of where the ends are at all times as they move quickly from side to side like whips and can harm your eyes.

FOR SPLITTING

As with knives, there are specific basketry tools for splitting cane and willow, known as cleaves. They cannot be found in shops but you can make them yourself or ask a skilled person to make them for you from wood or iron. They are made from iron or hard, compact wood, such as box.

Cane cleave: this is a cylindrical object with between three and nine channels from top to bottom, arranged around a central axis. These channels are partially

enclosed by the outside of the cleave (some are completely closed) to protect the hand from the cane's sharp edges. At one end of the cylinder, the channels join at the center and the walls that separate them are sharpened so that, after starting the separation with a knife, the cleave can be easily inserted and run through the length of the cane, tapping it to help the cleave pass through the nodes. The cleave must be hard enough to be able to stand up to these taps.

Willow cleave: made from a cylindrical piece of wood. At one end you can see a shape like a clover with concave, symmetrical leaves joined at the center. The channels between these gradually open out until they have disappeared at the other end of the cleave. At the center of the clover the cleave is slightly sharpened, so that it can be easily inserted into the grain of the wood and run along the stem to gently separate it.

Cane cleaves.

Willow cleave.

The characteristics of the available material will determine the techniques that can be used and the pieces which can be produced. Different basket making traditions have explored, often out of necessity, the limits and possibilities of each material and of each technique; however, there is still room for experiment. Some techniques are found in traditional basket making all around the world; others, on the other hand, are only found in one particular place.

basic Techniques

TECHNIQUES FOR WOODEN RODS

These are some of the techniques used in willow basketry. Willow and serge are amongst the most flexible of the wooden stems, which is why not everything that can be done with willow can be done with birch or hazel. For this reason it is a good idea to adapt and simplify the instructions here so that the material used is not forced and broken.

Round **cross base**

The Cross

This structure can be used as a base, a cover, as an object in its own right or as a starting point for a simple round piece. The weft consists of a cross-shaped frame; weavers are wound around this to hold the weft in place and to fill in the gaps left in the middle. This structure is almost universal, with some variations to cater to the differing flexibilities of the materials used.

When making a base, it is best to alternate the direction of the tips and the bases of the stems to harmonize the thicknesses in the framework as well as in the warp. To keep the shape as you go along, exploit the slight natural curve of the stems to shape the base, which should be convex so that the basket rests nicely on the ground. The stems used for the warp should be long and thin so that they can adapt to the demands of the moves that they have to make, especially in the central part of the cross.

1 Select and cut stakes of equal length a little longer than the desired diameter of the base; they should be the same size and more or less straight and smooth, cut from the thick part of the stem. In this case there are six stakes of about 25 centimeters in length but quantities and measurements can be adapted according to the material and the desired thickness of the weave.

2 With the knife, open up one of the stakes at the center (cleave the knife into the center and twist it to separate the grain of the wood).

3 Insert three stems into the gap.

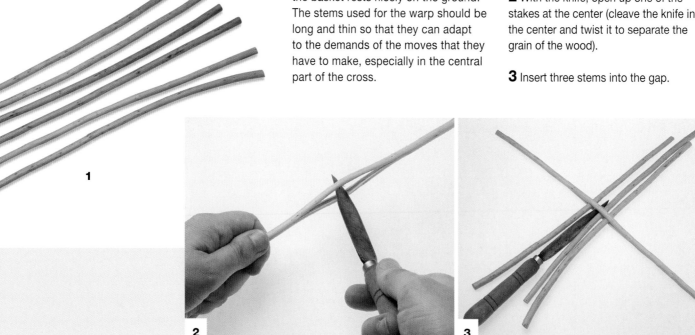

1

2

3

32

Twining the cross

Once the cross is made, it must be bound, or 'twined' while constantly pulling the stakes that are being bound so that the cross stays firm and regular throughout the process. When weaving, use your best hand to hold the weavers and to weave them, and then hold them in place with your least dextrous hand so that they don't move until the other weaver fixes them.

When the weavers become too thick or thin (so flexible that they don't provide any pressure), they need to be changed. To substitute a weaver leave it underneath, then insert another weaver of similar thickness; carry on weaving it but take it in the opposite direction. When a weaver runs out at the thick end, replace with a thick end and if it is at the thin end, replace with a thin end. The stiffness of the stem exerts pressure, which means that at the end it will not come undone. However, while the base is being woven, until another row has been completed, sometimes there are not enough fingers to hold all the stems in place.

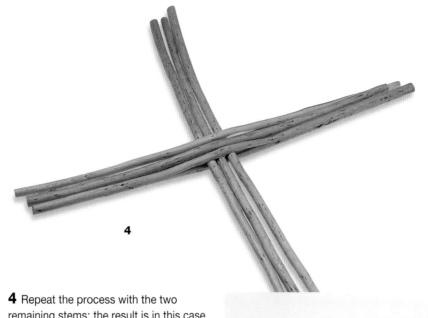

4

4 Repeat the process with the two remaining stems; the result is in this case a cross of three by three.

5 For the twining, choose two long thin stems and insert their ends in the hole in the cross.

6 Separate the stems, bend the first one (shown here in green) back on itself then take it over the first arm of the cross and leave it there without releasing it so that it does not come undone.

7 Take the second stem (shown here in white); after it has pressed down on and fixed the first step of the first weaver, take it over the second arm of the cross. There it will wait, held firmly, until the green one presses down on it and goes forward.

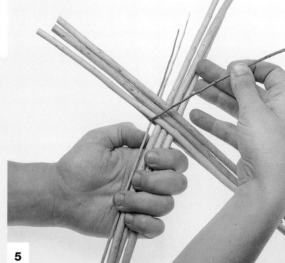

5

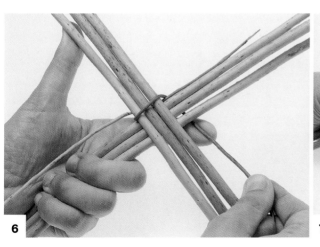

6

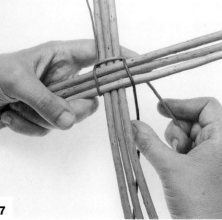

7

Separate the stems of the cross

When you have twined two or three rows around the heart of the cross, it is time to separate the three stems of each arm, which will be the framework for the base. Weave between each one to separate them, or if there is an even number, separate them into pairs first. Continue weaving in a forward direction, with the same weave, using two weavers that alternate and cross over each other, but now woven around just one stem for each step. The weavers (the warp) keep the stems of the weft separate, although it is important to strive to keep them parted so that the tips are positioned the same distance apart and at the same level. At this point, the stems that make up the star are known as 'spokes.' Carry on weaving rows, keeping the weave nice and even by joining thin ends to thin ends and thick ends to thick ends when weavers need replacing. Try to maintain a well-rounded, fairly convex shape with a thick and regular weave until the desired diameter is reached.

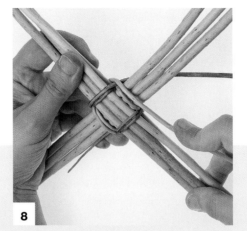

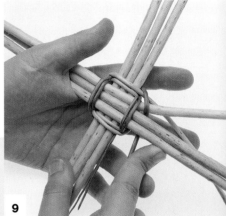

8

9

10

8 Two rows of twining are finished

9 Start to separate the stems of the cross that are to be the weft (spokes) of the base. Force them to one side and pass the weavers between them so that they separate.

10 The effort needed to keep the weavers as far towards the center as possible is considerable.

11 At the end of the first row around the cross, we are now left with a star shape and all the stems (now spokes) are separated.

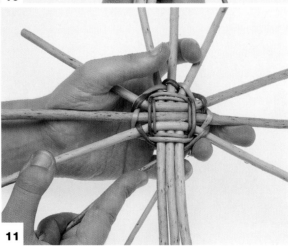

11

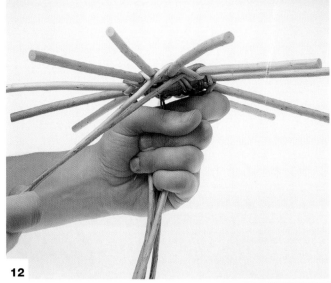

Finish the base

When the diameter is close to the desired size, in the last row of the weave try to ensure that the weavers are long enough to be able to complete an entire row and that they will finish at the thinnest end. This is especially important with the last weaver, or preferably the last two, to cut and tuck and ensure that the finished piece will be stable.

At this point, you can trim the ends that are in the way of the spokes and the weave, although it is best not to finish off yet because later on there will probably be some movement and stems may come out of place.

It is now time to adjust the final shape if it has not turned out perfectly; to do this, press it firmly between your feet, hands and knees.

At this stage, an object with this structure is only relatively stable. Once stakes have been attached to continue the shape of the basket, or to weave a rim around it, it is no longer in danger of coming undone.

12 By positioning the left hand close to the center of the cross as shown, you can maintain the desired shape and at the same time hold down stems as necessary, while the right hand manipulates the weaver that is moving in the forward direction.

13 You will need to keep changing the position of the fingers of your left hand to hold the weavers that are in play, especially after replacements.

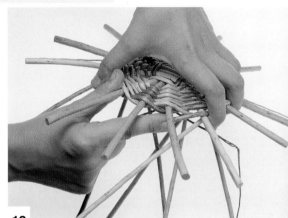

13

14

14 The last weaver, finished at the tip, completes the weaving of the base.

15 The base is now complete and any protruding ends may be trimmed.

15

Oval **cross base**

Structure

This is a variation on the previous base, with adjustments to make an oval shape. The cross has more arms, they are shorter than the spine and they are placed along this so that when the spokes are separated all their ends remain equidistant. In this example three stems have been used for the spine and six (two, one, one, two) for the arms. This frame is the most complicated to weave, especially at the beginning, because it is not easy to hold this many stems at the same time and achieve a regular result. Until the framework is fixed with the weave, the frame is not stable and once fixed it is too late to rectify any defects. The spokes of the frame are usually fixed by twining so that weaving can begin without the structure coming undone. In this case it has been bound with a willow stem split in two, which yields a finer and more flexible result than using it whole. To weave a more stable shape, it is a good idea to begin with two weavers at each end, which move in a forward direction two by two without ever catching on each other.

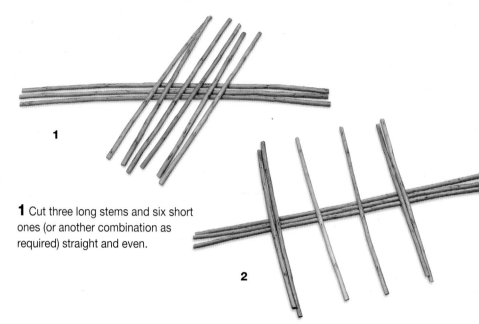

1 Cut three long stems and six short ones (or another combination as required) straight and even.

2 Cut a hole in the center of the short stems and feed the long ones through. Distribute the short stems evenly along the length of the long ones so that once separated the ends remain evenly positioned. In this case we have separated them into two, one, one and two.

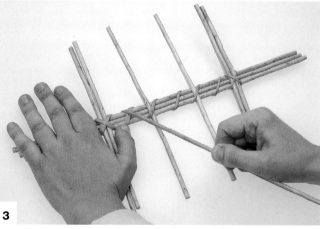

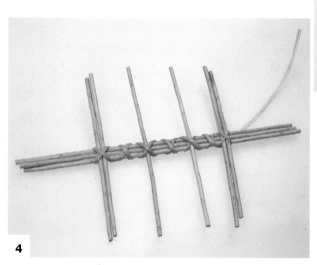

3 Fix the structure with a stem split in two, so that it is more flexible along its whole length and so that it does not bulge as much. Balance the two parts: begin twining at one end with one of the thin ends and at the other end with the other thin end.

4 The structure is now twined.

5 Begin to weave at one end of the frame with two long thin weavers.

6 Before reaching the other end, introduce another pair of weavers at that end.

7 Each one of the two pairs of weavers moves in a forward direction without ever catching each other. They complete two entire rows; one for each pair of weavers.

8 After completing the first two rows, separate the stakes at one end with one of the pairs of weavers.

9 Then separate the stakes at the other end, with the other pair of weavers. Then simply continue as for the round cross base.

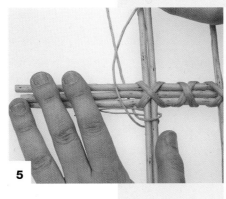

5

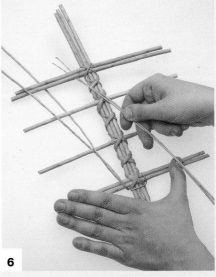

6

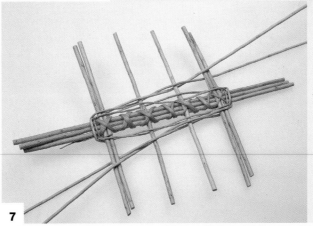

7

The warp

When a weaver is too thick, replace it. It is best not to make all the replacements in the same place; they should be distributed so that the securely woven parts reinforce the places where the weave is left broken by a join.

Again, perseverance is needed to keep the oval shape regular and quite convex and also to achieve a thick and regular weave.

It is not easy to find weavers that are long and thin enough to complete an entire row around a large base; in the last row it is important to try to leave all the ends finished so that they do not come undone.

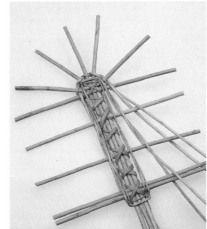

8

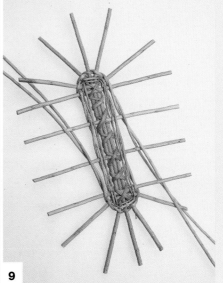

9

Flat **Round Base**

The hoop and the weft

This base is little known outside of its home, the eastern Iberian Peninsula. As well as frames known all over the world, such as the cross base and its variations, there are others, which may be more limited but are no less interesting for it. This frame is presented in this book because it is simple and has great aesthetic and creative beauty.
It has no protruding ends at the top or bottom; what's more, since it does not need the stakes to be attached (the stakes come out from the base) it makes pieces of great strength. To make this base, a single stem begins on one side of the base, crosses it, rises as a stake, then it is integrated into the rim or handle, eliminating the need for any additions. A basket made like this is very strong, much more so than one that needs joins.
It consists of one hoop, two sets of parallel lines that cross it and a series of weavers that are woven on this extremely simple structure without much manipulation, which stay perfectly fixed by their own tension.

1

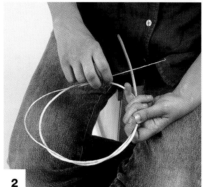

2

1 Take two long stems. Curve them without folding by sliding them along the front of the knee.

2 To establish the final perimeter of the base, make a hoop with the first stem by winding the weaver around on itself.

3 The second weaver is used to reinforce the hoop, twisting around it, maintaining an even thickness and following the grooves of the previous winding, as if it were a rope.

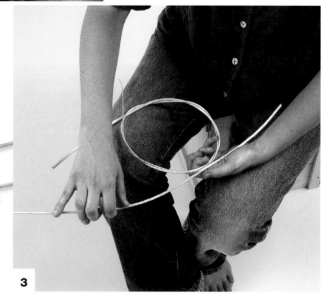

3

4

4 Place the hoop on the ground and place two parallel pairs of stems over it. These will form the weft in conjunction with the hoop. The layout that you can see in the illustration is just one option. It is important to try to keep to an even thickness. The thin ends should always be long and the thick ends always short (cut them if necessary).

The warp

The weavers for the base must be long, because they have a long distance to cover: their thickness at the base will determine their thickness at the handle or rim and this must be taken into account when choosing them; if they are too fine they won't reach the handle or they will make a flimsy rim, while if they are too thick, they will be very difficult to work. If the base is for a basket with a central handle, the first stems of the weft that are placed, the central ones, will need to be a little longer than the others, since they will make the handle later on. When it comes to weaving the base, there is no need for the weaver to make the whole journey (under, over, under, over): if you follow the example in the illustrations the task will be simpler and much faster. Also, as the weft is free at the top, it can join in the warp without losing shape. In reality, each weaver, once positioned, only has to make one move under a stake and the stake, as it is not fastened, can allow it to pass.

5 Hold the frame to the floor with your foot (you don't have to take your shoes and socks off) to keep it in place and begin the warp from the center at the widest part. Introduce the weaver between the stake on the left and the ring (from the point of view of the person working).

6 The rest of the weaver passes over the stake on the left and under the one on the right. This weaver has fulfilled its part of the warp and is now abandoned.

7 Take another weaver. Insert it into the weave of the base between the hoop and the stake on the right then pass the rest of it under the stake on the left. The second weaver is now finished. Now the basic framework is complete and you can rest your foot.

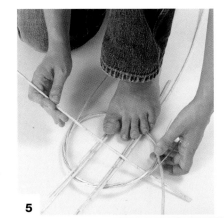

5

6

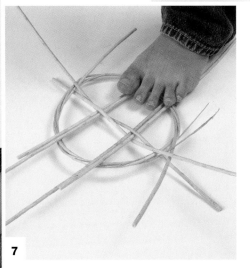

7

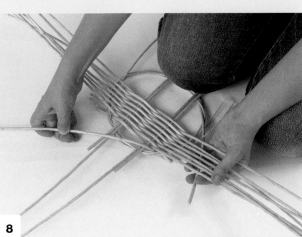

8

8 If a stem starts on the left and leaves on the right, the next one must start on the right and leave on the left. Continue weaving the first half of the hoop, moving forwards, a weaver to the left, one to the right, one to the left, one to the right... until you arrive close to the hoop.

9

Pack the filling

There is no need to have all the rods prepared and cut so that they are strictly uniform from the beginning; when placing them, insert them more or less into the base according to thickness, bearing in mind that the thickest part will be cut, and irregularity will disappear. As only the central part will be left visible, you should try to make this part nice and even.

So, with a new stem for each row, carry on towards the hoop. Before arriving at the hoop, turn the base (or the person working it can move to the other side) and weave the other half. Carry on filling the whole base, first one half, then the other, trying to keep the result regular, uniform, full or very full (it will contract and become looser when it dries) and concave (the smooth base is worked in reverse, and what is now concave, will be convex and stable once inverted). After forcing the last weavers into the warp (when it seems that no more will fit, there is still room for two or three more), also force the two stakes to join at the ends and that the whole base curves. Once the base is full, turn it upside down and cut the short tips so that they stay supported on the hoop; the tension exerted ensures that it will not come undone.

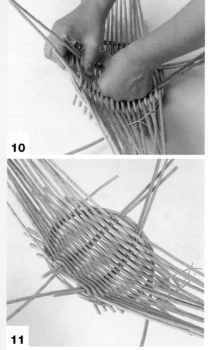

10

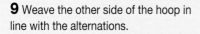

9 Weave the other side of the hoop in line with the alternations.

10 Fill the two sides in a little more, until there is no room left. Curve the base and bring the stakes together so that a couple more weavers can fit in. It needs to be very full and well rounded.

11 The base is now woven. The long ends will be the stakes, while the short ones will not be used.

12 Turn it upside down so that the short thick ends stay in the upper part. Cut these ends so that they are supported on the hoop but do not protrude more than a millimeter or two. Also cut the short ends of the stakes of the base.

11

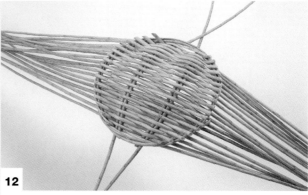

12

Flat **oval base**

A variant: the oval hoop

In this variation on the previous base, an oval shape is achieved by stretching a stem across the hoop. This 'rib' holds the shape of the hoop so that the force exercised by the weavers towards the outside does not make the base circular. The rib should be treated as part of the warp: when beginning to weave at its side, consider the rib as if it were another weaver when deciding the direction of those placed at its side, and if the rib ends up beneath a stake, the next shoot will pass above it, and vice versa.

From this point on, the base is no different from the round one. Again, you need to make a convex shape. The stems stay parallel, very regular and packed tight; the tips of the stakes join. Finally, turn it over and cut the thick ends.

A finished flat base, whether round or oval, can be used as part of a more complex piece or as a standalone piece: in this case, all the ends are cut and the piece does not come undone.

1 Use two stems to make a reinforced hoop, like the one for the round base. Choose another long fine stem.

2 Place the stem that is to be the rib right in the middle and starting at the end, attach it to the hoop by bending it back on itself and then twisting to fix it, and take it towards the other side. Stretch the hoop and fix the width of the oval with the rib. Twist the rib around itself from end to end three times to reinforce its hold.

3 The four stems of the weft are in position. One of the two pairs of stems is placed above the hoop and below the rib, and the other passes under the hoop and over the rib.

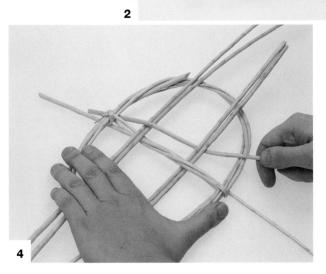

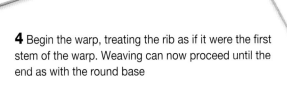

4 Begin the warp, treating the rib as if it were the first stem of the warp. Weaving can now proceed until the end as with the round base

Stakes

With a cross base

To weave the walls, you need a weft: the stakes. In cross based structures, the stakes of the wall are attached to the base. The stakes that form the weft of the walls will later form the trim, and in some cases, the handle. When choosing the stems you are going to use, ensure they are the right length and thickness. Choose with care because they must be in good condition all the way along, from end to end, and should all be more or less the same.

The number of stakes needed depends on the shape of the object, on how you want to weave the thickness of the wall (stakes closer together = thicker weave), on how you want the rim to be, the thickness of the stems and so on.

In this case two stakes have been inserted for each spoke of the base, amounting to 24. The stakes must be evenly spaced out around the outside of the base.

To attach the stakes, sharpen them at the thick end and push them into the weave, with the help of a bodkin so that once in, the stake will not come out. When all the stakes have been attached, the work resembles a sun

1

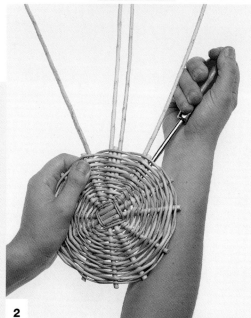

2

3

1 Sharpen a point at the thick ends of the stakes.

2 With a bodkin, make an opening for the stake next to a spoke and pull the bodkin out.

3 Immediately thrust the stake into the gap, as far in as possible.

At this point the basket maker needs more space around the piece being worked.

The next step is to bend the stakes up.

This is a delicate process because the stems must be bent upwards in a right angle without breaking them. One way of doing this is to insert the point of a knife in the place where we want the rod to bend (a few millimeters from the edge of the base, leaving space for one stem), with the blade following the direction of the grain of the wood. Then, give the knife a quarter turn at the same time as lifting the stake and this will help it to bend in this exact spot.

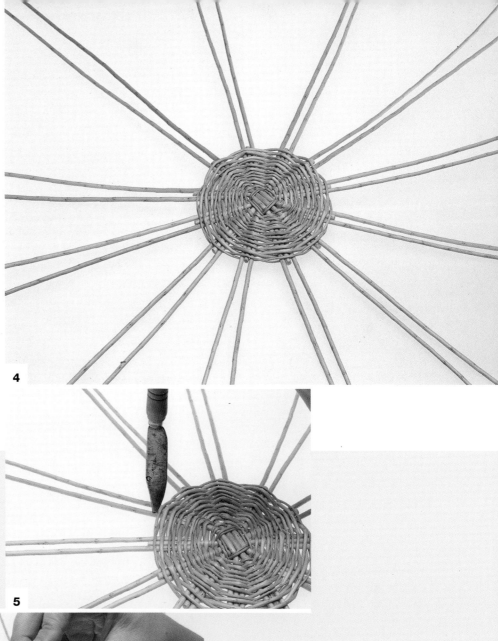

4

5

6

4 Position all the stakes. The result resembles a sun.

5 To bend the stakes at an angle without breaking them, insert the point of a knife following the direction of the grain of the wood, a few millimeters from the edge of the base.

6 Lift the stake at the same time as making a quarter turn with the knife.

7

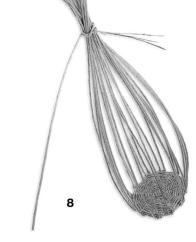

After bending, lifting and tying all of the stakes, they are now prepared for the warp that is about to begin. This moment of the creation is known as "the cage" and it really does look like one.

7 Once prepared, carefully bend the stakes up one by one, in an orderly manner.

8 Tie them at the top. This is the cage.

8

With a flat base

In the case of the flat base, the stakes just have to be attached at the ends: two stems must be inserted into the weave for each of the stakes in the base. The others do not need to be attached because they are already in place; they are the continuation of the weave of the base. Normally, four stakes are raised together for the part that will later become the handle, in other words the two central stakes have four stems, and the other stakes are raised in pairs—in other words, they are double stakes. This has consequences when making the rim as there will be more stakes in action. If it hasn't been done from the start, when the base is being woven, it is time to decide if there are too many stakes (the quantity that is necessary to weave the base is normally greater than the number of stakes needed) and to distribute those that you are going to keep permanently around the perimeter of the base when it is time to bend them upwards.

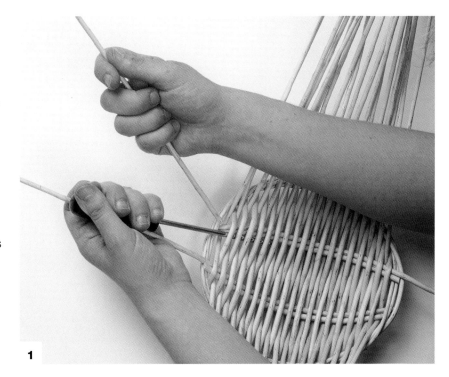

1

1 If you are using a flat base you only need to attach the stakes that are continuations of the those in the base, so that two groups of two come out of each end; the other stakes are already in place.

When bending the stakes upwards from the flat base, it is not necessary to mark them with the knife as the stakes do not form a right angle but instead go along the rim of the base. Following them carefully but firmly, with your fingers at the point where they bend, is enough. At this stage, you need to check that the shape of the base is convex; if it has bent the wrong way when the stakes have been bent upwards then it can be corrected by using your knee and foot to push it the right way, at the same time as using your hands to pull it in the opposite direction.

Now it is time to check the shape of the base,

2 Choose the strands which are going to be the stakes and bend them upwards carefully, leaving the others on the ground.

3 When bending the stakes upwards, choose and position them so that they are well spaced out around the rim of the base.

4 After, you will need to cut the leftover strands on the ground which were not chosen to be stakes, so that they support the rim of the base. Continue forming the base into a convex shape which should rest more on the edge than the center.

The **weave**

Two- and three-stem weave

These two patterns are woven with two or three weavers that will cross over each other and the stakes according to a strict pattern. It is normally used as embellishment for fixing a structure or at the end of a weave.

The first is in fact the fundamental pattern of the cross bases as explained in this book, and both can act as a weaving pattern for an entire object, or just a part of it. An entire object woven with two or three patterns (or more, but following the same rule) turns out thicker, heavier and more robust than one made with a coral weave and uses much more material.

One or two rows of a two- or three-weaver pattern, interwoven with a coral weave will protrude a little and break the uniformity of the whole, or hide a change in thickness. It looks like a rope wound around the piece and joined to the stakes. It combines utility (it lends firmness to the weave and the piece) with aesthetic interest.

These two-strand weaves are also used in the rim.

1 Start the two-strand weave: place the weavers at the base, behind two consecutive stakes.

2 Only one weaver is active at a time. The left-hand weaver overtakes the right-hand one and is passed behind the next stake, coming to rest on the right of the other weaver, which will be the next one to move.

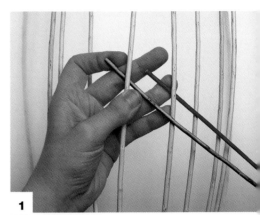

1

2

1 Start of the three-strand weave: place the bases of three weavers behind three consecutive stakes.

2 The weaver on the left overtakes the other two, passes behind the next stake and comes to rest on the right. The one on the left always goes ahead of the rest.

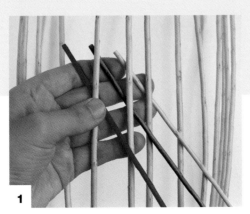

1

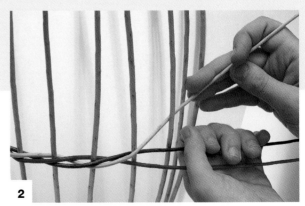

2

The rim

The section between the base and the wall is crucial to guarantee the strength of a piece. A rim is often woven here to hide the less decorative area/space of the intersection, to reinforce it, to adjust the separation between the stakes and to ensure that the piece sits well on its base without wobbling. The rim is woven with two or three weavers that will provide coverage and strength. This step is done when the stakes have been placed and bent upwards, in other words the cage has formed, but weaving the wall has not yet begun.

The rim needs to be bulky; for this a three-strand weave of thick weavers or three pairs of thinner weavers is ideal. When beginning the vertical weave, take this opportunity to cover the imperfections of the intersection with a two- or three-strand weave using a pair of stems as a single weaver.

Each time that a pair of weavers gets too thin, add in another pair. Add and substitute weavers as necessary to conserve the overall thickness.

1

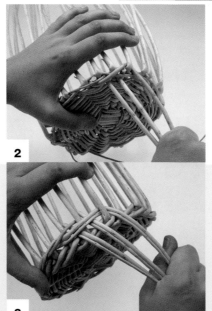

2

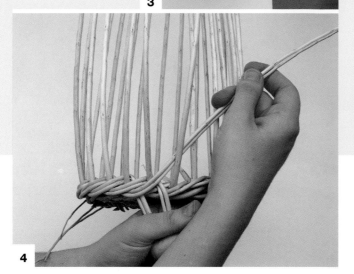

3

1 Sharpen three weavers and push them in from underneath, using a bodkin if necessary: the first after a stake, the second after the next stake and the third after the second.

2 Weave a whole row with three thick but flexible weavers (or doubles), forcing them to pass below the base.

3 On the second row, the rope passes touching the first to one side and begins to cover the intersection. One weaver has been added to each strand for greater coverage.

4 The second row is complete.

4

The third row can be worked with a two-strand weave after converting the three groups of two weavers into two groups of three.

When working this phase of a piece, it is crucial to ensure that each row is well fixed to the previous one and that the stakes remain well spaced and at the correct angle.

This is only one of the possible rims. Each type of base, each piece, may have its own but the general aims of the rim are: to give stability to the base, to add thickness to delay wearing out, to hide the less aesthetically pleasing aspects of the intersection, to aid the regular positioning of the stakes, and to add firmness of the structure...

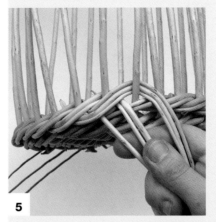
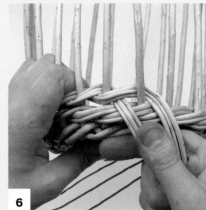

5 The three strands of two weavers are converted into two strands of three; the three-strand weave becomes a two-strand weave.

6 Work a whole row with a two-strand weave, with three weavers per strand, well positioned and flat, to give maximum coverage, adding extras where necessary.

7 When the whole row has been woven, it is finished. With a bodkin make a gap behind the weavers of the previous row.

8 Insert the tips into the gap and carefully pass the whole weavers through the gaps so that they do not fold.

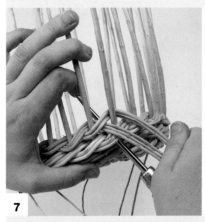

9 The rim is finished.

Coral weave

To weave a piece of basketry, once the stakes are in place there are many possible patterns. Apart from the intuitive weaves (behind, in front, behind, in front), and those in the previous pages, there is one, the coral weave, that offers beautiful results: regular, tight and uniform, it is fast to weave and requires little material. The warp consists of the same number of weavers as there are stakes and each one is woven at the same time as the others. The first few times it can seem complicated because of the large number of weavers in play, but it is easy to work once understood, and any errors are immediately apparent.

We have taken a red colored weaver to help demonstrate how to weave it. As shown in fig. 2, in order to pass the weaver behind the stake gently and without bending it, first pass the central part over it and then the tip.

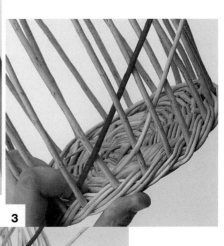

1 Choose as many weavers as there are stakes. They should all have similar lengths and thicknesses and the weavers should be finer than the stakes.

2 and **3** Take one and place its base between two stakes.
Pass the rest in front of one and behind the next (moving towards the right) and leave it (for now). Take another (shown here in red) and do the same, placing it to the left of the first.

4 Weave the rest like this: always placing weavers to the left, while the weave continues towards the right. Eventually, the last weaver will be under the one that started. One weaver should come out from each space between stakes.

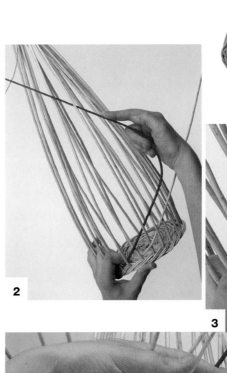

Once all the weavers are in place, it is just a question of weaving them, one by one but all at the same time: in front of one stake, behind the next and leave it. Take the left hand weaver and take it in front of one, behind the next and leave it. Continue like this, weaver by weaver and row by row. If a weaver breaks, it can be substituted for another of the same thickness at that point, hiding the change in the least visible part, in other words, behind a stake.

Continue the weave until you reach the desired height or until the weavers are so fine that they can no longer be used. They should all end at the same height, so that after one entire row; they are cut one by one, one behind each stake (which can hold it in place).

With this method of weaving, all the weavers of this woven band will lose thickness at the same time, the joins will concentrate in one single line and the general aspect is of a job well done.

5 While weaving, try to control the shape of the piece, the path of each weaver (which should not displace the stakes) and the thickness of the weave, tightening it frequently with the hands.

6 Tools can be used to tap the weave and make it denser. Once it is dry, it will loosen.

7 When a band is finished, cut each weaver behind a stake to support it. If you want to carry on weaving, repeat the beginning: place as many weavers as there are stakes in place and continue weaving in the same manner.

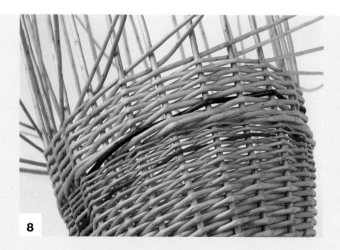

8 When splicing there is a variation you can use exploiting the initial thickness of the new weavers: in the first row, pass them in front of two stakes instead of one. Afterwards, weave as normal.

The finish of the weave is made with the stakes and forms the rim of the basket. After taking the weft and incorporating it with the warp in this manner, it is impossible to carry on weaving, and at the same time it means that the warp cannot escape from where it has been placed. Apart from the decorative purpose, which is a bonus, the aim of the rim is to cut and tuck the object so that it does not come undone.

The flat finish

There are many different ways of making a border. The most simple in rod basketry is to bend and insert each stake next to the following stake, or pass it behind the next one and once the row is finished, with only one move per stake (each one stays fixed by the next), trim the ends.
Some wood will not allow more than this, but willow, being so flexible, has many possible finishes, which can be very tough as well as decorative.
The flat finish is a little more elaborate. Here we will explain how to make the most simple version: the flat finish, behind one and in front of two.

1 Provisionally place a piece of stem next to the base of a stake and lower the stake over the stem (to simulate the thickness of the stem that will finish the rim) and behind the next stake.

2 Pass the second stake behind the following one, and do the same with the third, in other words pass each stake behind the following one.

3 Take the first stake that was lowered, pass it front of two stakes and bring it out from behind the third. The first stake that is still upright, is then lowered to the side of this last one.
This one (shown here in blue) is the first to have completed its journey: behind one, in front of two.

1

2

3

4

4 The lowered stake that is furthest to the left passes in front of two stakes and comes out behind the next one and finishes there. Lower the first upright stake next to it down behind the next one and wait.

Basic techniques

This is the simplest version of this type of rim: behind one and in front of two. Modifying the pattern (behind two and in front of five; behind one and in front of three, etc.) changes the final appearance quite a lot, but the basic technique is the same and when this is understood, you can try making other variations.

Each stake makes its journey in two phases: first it is bent down and passed behind the stake to its right. Then it waits and later when there are two more bent over to its right (in front of two, two bent over stakes) these two move forward and are placed next to the following one where they will finish.

When a stake has passed in front of two, it has accomplished its second task; the first upright stake makes its first move (behind one), passing by the same place, to the side. Now there will be two stems left together, of which one is finished (the one on the left) and the other is awaiting its turn: when there are two more bent over stakes to its right.

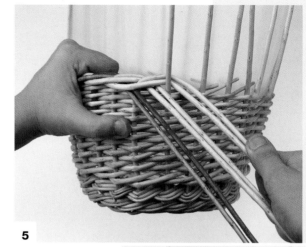

5

5 The one on the left passes in front of two stakes and is positioned after the third. The first upright stake is lowered behind the next stake. This is the first part of its path.

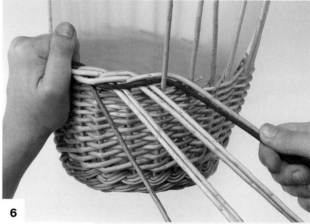

6

6 Here, three pairs of weavers are lowered in action: this is the regular position (not starting or finishing) when working this rim. Of each pair the one on the left is abandoned because it has finished its journey and the one on the right has only finished the first part: it still has to pass in front of two and leave behind the following stake.
At its side another stake is lowered.

7 This pattern continues until there is only one stake left upright

7

At the end of the row, in the last steps, the stems cannot simply bend and move, because to their right, the other stems are already bent. Even so, nothing changes in their path, they just have to be inserted between the stakes that are already bent over and interlaced. The difficulty now is mechanical: a bodkin is useful to help insert the point and then push them in from behind so that in passing between the stems, they continue in a curve and don't get folded. When making a flat rim, in the first stage, the first stakes are bent over (if it is in front of two, three stakes). In the second stage, in each step there is a stem that finishes on accomplishing its second task and one that finishes on accomplishing its first. Finally, when all have made their first move, the only thing left is for the last ones (who were the first to bend over) to complete the second move, which will be done by inserting them between the others.

8

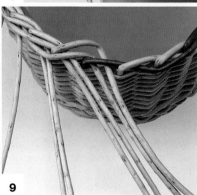

9

8 Next, the stems that are still to make the second step, having passed in front of two and come out from behind the next stake, will find that this next stake has already been lowered. However, they can still pass behind it and come out from underneath and so the pattern is maintained.

9 The last upright stake is bent down to the side and passes under the rim. In these last steps, rather than pulling the end, take care where the stem has been bent so that it doesn't break or make a visible fold.

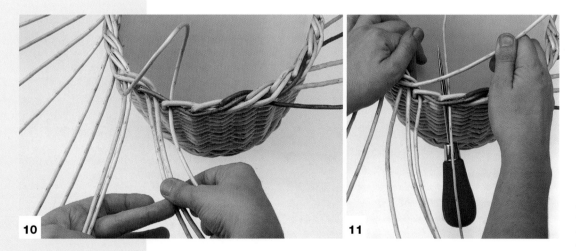

10

11

10 The first task is complete. The only thing left to do is pass the three last stems in front of two and bring them out behind the next.

11 With a bodkin open up a gap between two already woven stems and immediately insert the stem.

When the rim has been finished, all the ends must appear perfectly distributed between the stakes, never folded, and there should be no gaps. If this isn't so, there must have been a mistake. During the completion of the rim, it is important to control the general shape of the piece and the height of the rim. Taking into account that the willow will shrink when dry, the border should be made as low as possible so that it looks like a continuation of the weave and there should be no spaces left between the weave and the rim. It is also a good idea to make sure the last steps of the finish do not look too different from the rest. Some defects can be rectified with a few taps of the awl or mallet or just using your hands.

When cutting the ends you don't need to make them very neat yet, as the contraction of the wicker when dry, combined with the possible movements of later steps can mean that some ends could come loose. It's best to finish off when the piece is completed and dried.

12

13

12 This is the last move of the rim. When finished, a stem comes out from behind each stake.

13 The protruding ends can now be trimmed.

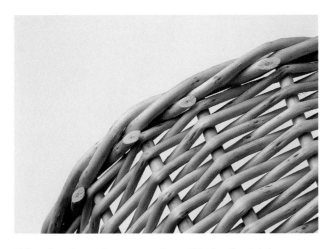

If there is to be another stage, such as adding handles, it is better not to finish off.

Here you can see the path of the stems of the finished rim: in the first stage they pass behind one and in the second stage in front of two (and come out after the next one).

The rope embellishment

This finish looks like a rope wound around the rim of the piece, and this is what it actually is: a rope made from the stakes that are incorporated as it goes around the opening of the piece. It is not as precise a process as the flat rim, as it is harder to maintain regularity when not using stakes. It requires strength, skill and practice and once started, it cannot be put down until it has been finished. In the whole of the embellishment, we are working with three groups of stems which are twisted around each other, and as each group passes it fixes the twist of the previous row.

In this example, the embellishment is made after the handle, which is also made using the rope method. It begins at the side of the handle that has already been made from two stems, adding a stem to the stake.

1 Attach a stem to reinforce the first stake after the handle. This will be the third strand of the rope, together with the two from the handle. The three strands are of the same thickness.

2 Separate the two strands of the rope which arrive from the handle. Now, try to make it look as if the rope were continuous and pass it in front of the first stake, leaving the first strand inside the piece between the first and second stakes.

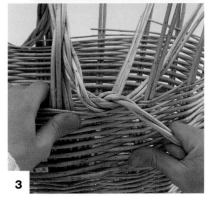

3 Twist the other strand that comes from the handle and leave it inside the piece, before the next stake. Immediately, take the first stake, twist it and lean it over. Two strands are left free inside, and the third outside, well supported.

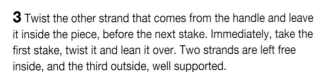

4 Slide and twist the bundle that you have in your hand as you move it towards the inside of the piece, passing it between the two weavers of the following stake: at the same time, take the free strand of the rope from the far left, twist and incorporate the first weaver of the stake, take it outside and press it downwards to fix the previous step.

The method is now regular: there are two strands inside the piece and a third outside, supported by the hand. This strand is twisted and goes inside the piece (once between the stake's stems, the next between the stakes). At the same time that the first strand from inside picks up a stem from the stake, it is twisted and goes towards the outside, presses on and fixes the previous move. The strand that goes outside the piece with each step is held with the left hand and is responsible for attaching the rope that is being made to the edge of the basket. The stakes that are being incorporated, stem by stem, attach the finish firmly to the rest of the piece. The right hand takes the strand from the left hand, twists it and takes it to a space: you can place it inside the piece after the next stem and can skip it since the strand that arrives from inside fixes this movement as it comes out.
Try to maintain the thickness of each strand by leaving ends inside the piece, before incorporating the stake.
When the rope is being made, the first difficulty is crossing the handle.

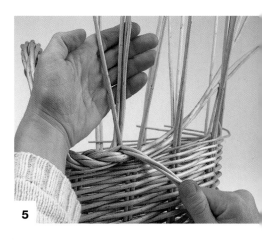

5

5 The left hand picks up a strand from inside, incorporates a stem and keeps the rope in place (just on top of the wall and well-fixed underneath), while the right hand twists the strand from outside and takes it forward a step.

6

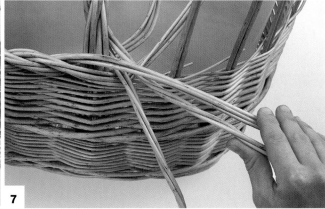

7

8

6 When you arrive at the handle, there are three strands that belong to the rim (two are inside and one outside) and two with the handle. The first group of the rim passes in front of the handle and enters just afterwards.

7 The second group of the rim also passes in front of the handle and joins with one of its groups. They are twisted together.

8 They are placed between the weavers of the following stake. This movement is secured by the group that comes next, which is the third strand of the rim, which comes from behind the handle, joined with the second group that came from the handle.

Once the techniques for this finish are understood, the objectives are to maintain the thickness of the rope, to ensure that it is well positioned (attached to the end of the previous weave and in line with it, following the line of the rim), ensuring that the twist is always even. To maintain the thickness of the rope, leave stems inside the piece as you go along.

When picking up the strands from the inside of the piece and taking them outside, gauge the thickness of the strand with your fingers and only take those necessary. Until you have had more practice, it will suffice to have a determined number of stems in each strand, or one more if they are very fine. So that the rope stays well positioned on the rim, you will have to balance out the tendency of the strands to deviate towards the inside of the piece, which happens because of the resistance of the strand which pushes towards the outside. This can be achieved with an added stake. If the two moves are done at the same time, one with each hand, it is easier to control them. Another tendency that you will have to combat is where the rope doesn't attach well to the wall and stays raised. All the twists of the rope trim has to be done taking these tendencies into account and combatting them by pressing downwards and making all the movements very level with previous ones.

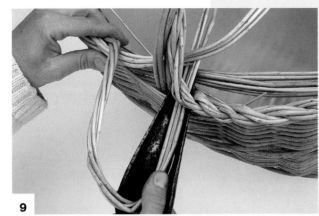

9 The second half is worked like the first, up until you arrive at the handle once more: this is the end.
Carry on twisting; the first strand that will need to be placed after the handle is between the two main ropes of the handle. From this point, the awl will be essential.

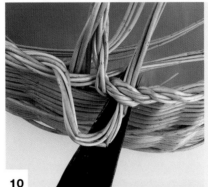

10 The next strand, after passing in front of the handle, is inserted into a space further along.
On top two twisted strands remain.

11 The last strand, which passes behind the handle, exits immediately afterwards, twists and is inserted into the following space, under the twisted strands.

12 When the finish is complete, the ends can be cut.

The **handles**

Rope handles

This type of handle is usually combined with a rope trim. It is made before the trim (although this isn't the only way of doing it) so that you can incorporate the ends that are left over in the rim and this makes it appear as though the rim and handle is made from one rope that goes all around the piece and carries on over the center to form the handle.

Usually, in a piece with a central handle the central stakes have more stems than the rest: they have already been placed like this at the base (in the case of a flat base) or the stakes have already been inserted into the weave (in a cross base).

3 The six are divided into two groups of three. Twist the first clockwise from base to tip. Then twist the second in the same way.

4 Cross the two strands. Begin to pass left in front of right and continue in the same direction until you reach the tips of the stems. Tie them so that they do not unravel then repeat the process on the other side of the piece.

1 Starting with a basket with the stakes still upright, with four stems to each stake that is to be included in the handle.

2 Sharpen and attach two more weavers in each side so that there are now six per side.

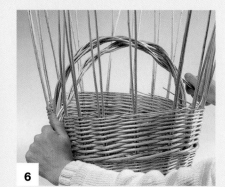
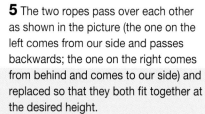

2

5 The two ropes pass over each other as shown in the picture (the one on the left comes from our side and passes backwards; the one on the right comes from behind and comes to our side) and replaced so that they both fit together at the desired height.

6 The piece is ready to begin the trim.

3

4

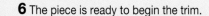
5

6

Wrapped wooden handle

This handle consists of a central piece of willow, cut to size and inserted down into the weave on each side next to two stakes. This piece of willow gives shape and stiffness to the handle and is wrapped in stems that cover it and secure it to the structure of the piece. The most visible part of the handle (the height, the shape) isn't the only important thing: the piece of willow must stay securely attached to the inside of the piece on both sides. For this, you need to sharpen both ends and open a gap up with a thick bodkin and pass them through.

You can take advantage of the fact that the handle is added at the end when the piece is finished, by using it to hide imperfections or any asymmetry that have arisen during the making of the basket. It is not unusual for the last stems of the rim to look angular or irregular; if the shape of the piece allows, the handle can be attached next to them so that these imperfections are hidden by the join. It is also time to re-establish symmetry if it has become a little skewed during the weaving process: attaching the handle to one side of a well-chosen stake can partially correct the problem.

1

2

1 For the center of the handle, choose a willow stem of the correct thickness; curve it by sliding along the front of the knee. Cut it to size; sharpen both ends to a point with a knife and insert both ends down into the weave next to two opposing stakes, ensuring that it is central.

2 Choose four finer stems (with another combination of thicknesses, the amount can be different), sharpen at the base and insert these down into the weave on the left of one of the sides of the handle. Using a bodkin is essential to this task.

3 Wrap them along the length of the handle so that they cover the start of the exterior part and wrap them around it three times. So that they don't get bent, pass the central part over first and then the tip.

3

4 The stems must be well positioned, flat and well distributed along the length of the handle.

4

After attaching the handle, choose the pieces of willow that will cover it. They should all be the same and very smooth so that the piece can be carried comfortably. They need to be long enough to be attached to one of the sides: wrap around the handle and make a knot at the other side.

In its path from one side of the piece to the other, the stems that cover the handle will wrap around it three times. They are worked together: try and keep them flat and without folds by passing first the central part and then the tips over the handle and leave them at the end for tying. Sometimes, after twisting the stems along and around the handle, there is still space for one or two more. These can be inserted into one of the sides. Try to maintain symmetry and make the added stems cover the space that has been left.

The nature of the handle's curved shape means that the stems have to cover a longer distance on the top than underneath, which means that some space is left on the top and the wrap is tighter underneath. This is normal and there is no need to use too many to try and cover the handle completely—if this means leaving protruding stems underneath; since this is where the basket will be supported by the hand, it would make it uncomfortable to carry.

5

6

5 With the help of a bodkin, insert four more pieces of willow, sharpened with a knife, into the other side of the handle, in the same way as the first side.

6 Wrap them around the handle, filling in the gaps left by the weavers from the other side.

7

8

7 The handle is completely covered. If there is some uncovered space, more stems can be added to one of the sides and wrapped with the rest to perfect the result.

8 A bodkin, or even better, an awl will help to pass the ends towards the outside to start tying the handle to the piece.

There are many different ways of binding the handle to the piece; we will only explain one of them here. The important thing about the binding, apart from how it looks, is that it is fixed correctly to the handle; without this knot it would only be inserted into the weave of the basket, which means that it could be pulled out with a yank or by a sufficiently heavy load. For this reason, when choosing the weavers to wrap the handle, it is important to check that they are long enough so that the binding will be secure. This is a central handle; if you want to make a little handle at the side, so that the basket can be lifted with one hand, the stems that cover it will have to be twisted first, following a specific technique, so that they lose their stiffness and are flexible enough to wrap around the handle; a more demanding task with the shorter handle.

There is an example of this in one of the pieces demonstrated in the step-by-step guides.

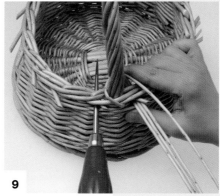

9

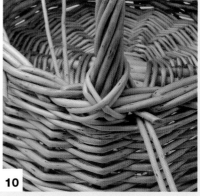

10

9 This binding is done with the stems, one by one. The first crosses the handle and trim diagonally, passes behind the base of the handle and returns to enter the piece on the left.

10 Repeat the process with the other stems. Try to ensure that they are well positioned and do not fold.

11 To finish the binding, pass the stems under the rim, first towards the outside and then towards the inside, tucking them behind a stake.

12 Now the ends can be trimmed.

11

13

12

13 Repeat the process on the other side. The piece is now finished and can be trimmed.

Basic techniques

TECHNIQUES FOR MORE FLEXIBLE MATERIALS

These are some of the techniques that can be applied to straw, rush, and palm leaves or esparto, which are all more flexible than willow.
We will not show the more intuitive ones or those similar to textile techniques here, where weft and warp are crossed at varying distances and alternations. We will only show some actual basketry techniques that are primarily indicated for natural materials.
By combining techniques and materials you can play around with the beauty and functionality of the pieces.

The **stitched coil**

This basketry technique seems to be the oldest and most widespread of all. The filling and stitching materials can be different or the same. Usually, a cheap and easy to find material is used for the filling, such as straw and grasses, and especially long and flexible material for stitching, such as strips of bramble, very fine strips of split willow, raffia, large fibrous leaves, etc. In fact even the rope maker's shop can provide materials for stitching.

By using different materials and sewing with different stitches, combining sewing materials and colors, all kinds of pieces can be obtained, from the crudest to the finest, including some that are so dense and well-made that they can even hold liquids.

In this example, you can see the start of a coil made with fine straw as filling and raffia as stitching material. The stitch is only one of various types possible and probably the most simple, but it will do to start practicing this technique.

1 Take a bundle of straw of the desired thickness. Start wrapping the raffia around one end of the straw, ensuring that the start is covered and secured by the wrapping and that the straw is well covered.

2 When there is a sufficient amount of covered straw to make a small ring (the measurements depend on materials and thicknesses) start the coil.

A variant on the stitched coil uses the same material for the filling and the stitching. For example, if it were made of straw, only the pieces of stem from next to the ear would be used. With each stitch the current row is fixed to the previous one, wrapping around the filling. It is a detailed and delicate job. Other possibilities are combining colors or stitching materials, or working with different types of stitch: some leave the filling visible (its color, shine, thickness of the pieces) and others cover it completely, so that the texture of the final piece is only that provided by the stitching material. At first it seems a very simple technique, but it does, in fact, offer a whole range of possibilities using a lot of materials.

3

3 The bundle of straw is twisted to conserve its circular section and so that it does not chafe with the stitching, and also to soften the bending of the coil and avoid folds.

4 With each stitch, bind the straw to the one before it.

4

Example of stitched coil.

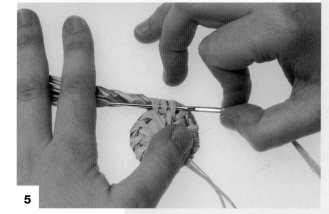

5

5 To introduce new stitching material use the pressure of the already sewn part to hold the new piece in place, as well as the bundle of straw and the sewing material that has not been used but is too short to continue. It can be cut after they have crossed. Also you will need to add straw to the bundle to maintain thickness when pieces end. A small ring can act as a guide.

Braids and **plaits**

When working with material directly extracted from plants, the main difficulty is that leaves or stems or whatever you're working with must be replaced very often without the weave becoming weak at this point. As long as straw or esparto may be, they will not be longer than a couple of handspans. Braids and plaits are a way of indefinitely lengthening the base material, making a single strip from cut pieces. This is solid because the succession of splices reinforces it in its entirety.

The braid or plait can be stitched in a coil to make all kind of objects; they have flexibility different from material used directly and most importantly they are much stronger. A braid of three strands is something that everybody knows how to do and is generally considered to be the most simple of plaits.

For example, rushes can be worked in a three-strand braid and then stitched into a coil.

The rush is thick and a three-strand braid offers a considerable thickness that is usually stitched in a stack: the face of the braid can only be seen in the rim of the piece.

1

1 Start a plait of five (in this case, made with unsplit palm leaves): a vertical leaf and two leaves crossed on top.

2 The vertical leaf bends forwards.

4

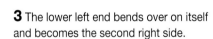

3

Vintage esparto scouring pads

3 The lower left end bends over on itself and becomes the second right side.

4 The lower right end bends over on itself and becomes the left side. Five ends are left pointing towards the front.

With more than three pieces (four, five, seven, nine, eleven) you can weave broad flat strips, as long as needed. The only requirement is that the material should be flexible and long: long and fibrous leaves, straw, esparto (which is worked in groups of stems), etc. Here we are showing only two types of plait, but there are many more: broader, with other patterns of crossovers, with serrated edge, with curves included in the weave... The plait can be very fine or very robust, according to the quantity of material used to weave it: one palm leaf will not have the strength of three leaves together. Given that you will be working with several pieces at the same time try and spread out the substitutions of material (pieces that end and have to be replaced), so that the plait looks clean and regular and ends up strong. Each material has its own characteristics when it comes to joining.

5

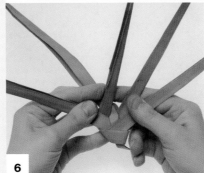
6

5 The first strip on the left (the one that is furthest towards the back) is bent downwards and passes under its neighbour...

6 ... and over the center leaf.

7

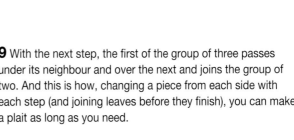
8

7 The first on the right is bent downwards and passes under its neighbour..

8 ... and over the center leaf. There is now a group of three (on the left) and a group of two (on the right).

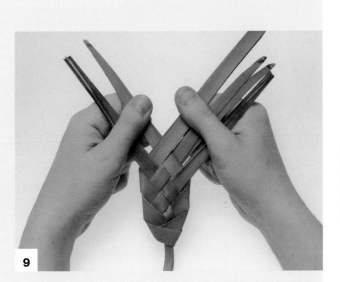
9

9 With the next step, the first of the group of three passes under its neighbour and over the next and joins the group of two. And this is how, changing a piece from each side with each step (and joining leaves before they finish), you can make a plait as long as you need.

Plaits with odd numbers of pieces are good for stitching into a coil; if you wish to make a beautifully presented piece, the result will look a lot like an intact weave without additions.

Plaits with even numbers of pieces are used as decorations or for objects that are not worked in a coil.

Making a plait is a mechanical and entertaining job that could be considered as preparation of material for making large objects without having to directly manipulate a material that often makes the task interminable.

Mats, carrycots, covered or uncovered pieces, small or large, very fine or very strong pieces, large or small containers, bags, hats, games or decorative objects...these are all possible applications for plaits of different materials.

1 A seven strand plait, with three unsplit leaves per strand: there are three strands on one side and four on the other.

Little toy donkey: plait reinforced with wire.

2 The first on the left (beginning from behind) passes under one and over two, and joins the other group.

3 The first on the right also passes under one and over two, and joins the other group. Continue in this manner, adding leaves as needed so that the thickness stays regular. The plait can be made as long as needed.

This shape is made from a cross shaped structure filled with material that must be flexible enough to wind around the arms of the cross without breaking. Soaked straw can be used: in the photographs you can see a piece of straw shaping the rhombus over a rigid cross of dry willow, although the cross can also be made of straw or other material. If woven on a solid structure, the result will have the stiffness of dry straw in the walls combined with strength provided by the solid frame. It is possible to create different volumes and shapes by using this technique and varying the structure. Although it won't support much weight, it is beautiful.

This technique is also used for binding frames with ribs: typically made with hazel or fine willow strips, which are rigid materials but when split or cut into strips they gain much flexibility in one direction without the wood losing strength. The ribs of the frame are held securely in place by the rhombus. This type of piece, using these materials, held in place by the rhombus is capable of bearing heavy loads.

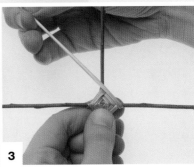

1 The structure consists of two crossed pieces of willow and a piece of straw is placed in the center ready to weave.

2 The piece of straw completes a turn around each consecutive arm of the cross, continuing until the rhombus appears.

3 After completing a turn around the one on the right it is prepared to go around the uppermost arm.

4 Now go around the arm on the left. Then wind it around the bottom arm. If joins must be made, the angles will be useful for fixing and concealing changes.

Rhombus structure in hazel piece.

The **helix**

With this technique you can make a long even rope, cup shaped pieces or pieces that first get wider and then narrower until they close. They are usually made with straw but soaked willow will work too. This technique is most often used for small decorative objects or embellishments for other pieces but is also used to make rattles, dolls and much more.

The main difficulty with this work is the joins, which is why this technique is usually only used for small pieces that use whole stems, without joins, and then pieces can be joined together if necessary.
In the case of straw rope, splices can be made in the bends, inserting one piece of straw inside another.

The example shows a coil with four sides woven with five pieces, but they can be made with six sides (seven pieces) or more.

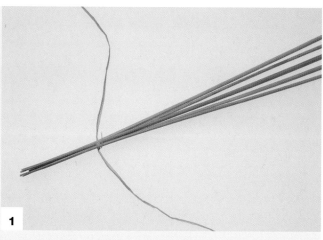

1

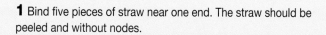

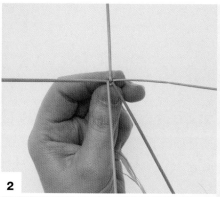

2

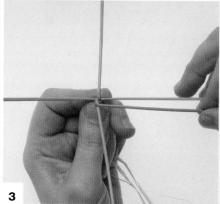

3

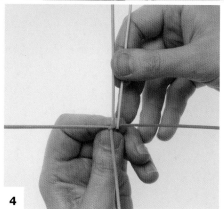

4

1 Bind five pieces of straw near one end. The straw should be peeled and without nodes.

2 Arrange four of the pieces in the shape of a cross, pointing towards the north, south, east and west (to make sure we understand each other), and the fifth piece lies in a south-easterly direction.

3 The fifth piece goes back and passes around the one that is lying in a southerly direction and comes to rest above it at the east side, without moving it forwards.

4 Leave the one that has just moved forward, which should now be to the east. The piece that was previously the easterly one is the one to move next: it goes back, passes around the new easterly piece and it comes to rest next to the northerly piece, without moving it forward.

The best materials to work with using this technique are flexible enough to withstand being twisted, which is demanding as far as flexibility is concerned. At the same time, they must be stiff enough to maintain a fairly rigid shape once they are dry. In other words, the materials need to be rigid when dry and flexible when moist. Straw and willow are perfect in these terms, but there are more materials that will work.

To make a rattle, insert stones, husks, shells, etc. into the piece before closing it, so that once it is finished, the objects that make the sound do not come out.

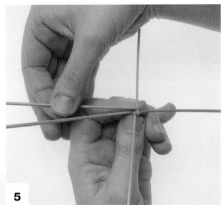

5

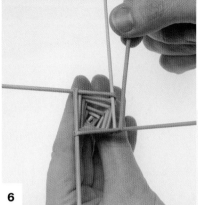

6

5 Leave the piece that has just moved to the north and take the one that was in that position. Pass it around the recent arrival and place it to the west. Then leave it there. The next one to move is the one that is now in the west.

6 Each piece passes behind the previous one and is put in the following position where it waits and the one that was there makes the next move.

7 Continue in this manner; the object will open out and ridges will form in the shape of a helix, until the desired width is achieved.

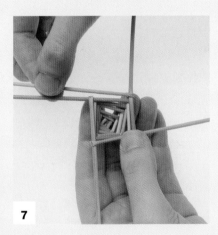

7

The same, but made from willow. Here the piece is closing: the stem that moves forward is placed a little after the one that it has met, so that the perimeter of the square is getting smaller.

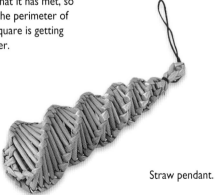

Straw pendant.

Step
by step

To act as a guide or to give you inspiration, you will be shown here how to make five objects with different materials: wicker or rattan, reeds, palm fronds and chestnut bark. The complete process is explained from the beginning, including the preparation of the material, right through until the completion of the piece. You will see how the basic techniques vary slightly in the hands of different artisans.

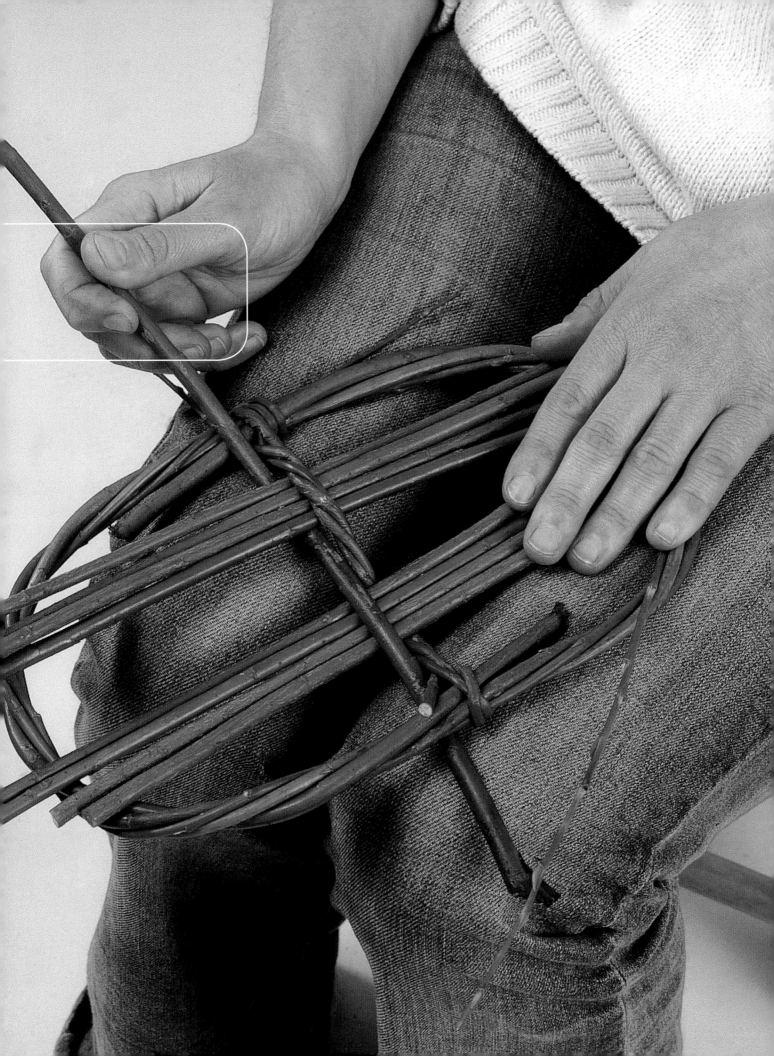

A plaited
palm **pannier**

With a stylized shape and made with palmetto leaves, this basket has the smell, the crunch, the color and the texture of natural palm. The palm has previously been moistened and braided into a plait of nine strands of three whole leaves each. Some leaves dyed with vegetable dyes have been incorporated into the finish to provide a delightful contrast with the more discreet green of the dry palm. The piece weighs one kilogram, which gives an idea of the quantity of palm leaf needed and also of the robustness of this version of the traditional moses basket. Work by Raquel Serres and Rosario Vidiella.

1 The first job is to make the plait. For this piece it will need to be six times the length of the distance between your hands with open arms.

2 To begin to shape the base a leaf is threaded through a needle and knotted at the end. It is then passed under one of the central strands near the beginning of the plait

3 Pass the needle between the two knotted ends so that the stitch does not slip out.

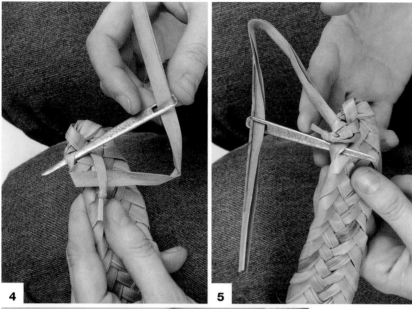

4 Then take out the needle from under the strand on the edge of the plait.

5 And push it back in by the next strand.

6 Fold the beginning of the plait and pass the needle under the strand at the edge. Now the coil is beginning to form. Make three stitches on alternate sides, towards the center of the coil.

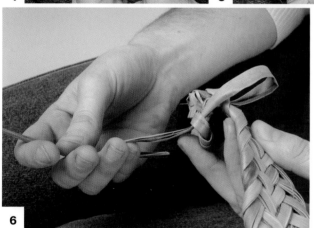

7 Go back to the edge of the plait and pass the needle under three strands along the edge, to keep the coil moving in the right direction.

8 Now pass it under the starting strand of the plait and force this start of the coil to flatten out.

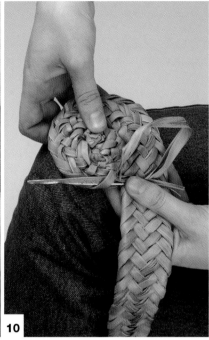

9

10

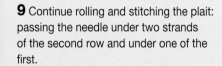

9 Continue rolling and stitching the plait: passing the needle under two strands of the second row and under one of the first.

10 Flatten the center of the coil by forcing it down with your fingers, and continue sewing, spreading out the stitches. The leaf that is used for stitching cannot be seen; it alternates by passing once inside and once outside, under one strand or two, according to the coil which is being shaped.

11 This is a good way to keep the plait that is waiting to be stitched: rolled up next to the work chair.

12 The base is the right size when it has the same diameter as the plait that is still rolled up waiting to be worked. "Flatten the center of the coil by forcing it down with your fingers, and continue sewing, spreading out the stitches."

"Flatten the center of the coil by forcing it down with your fingers, and continue sewing, spreading out the stitches."

11

12

13

13 To make the angle between the base and the wall, the new plait should be placed at the desired angle to the base, then sewing can continue, alternating the stitches in the coil and in the new plait being joined to it.

14

15

14 Here part of the first row of the wall has been stitched in place and the new angle of the plait takes shape.

15 The artist keeps the knees raised so the piece is kept in a stable and comfortable position to work.

"The base is the right size when it has the same diameter as the plait that is still rolled up waiting to be worked."

16 The leaves being used for sewing from top to bottom are joined with this splice. When a piece is finished, pass the tip of a new one behind it...

17 ... then it gives a forward twist to the left, passes behind then exits in front of the little finger.

18 It goes around the little finger, passes behind the piece coming from the basket and exits through the first loop that it has made.

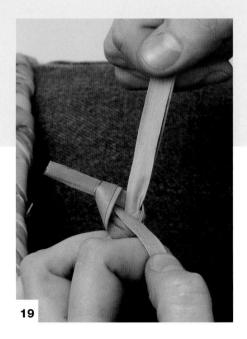

19 The two ends are pulled and stitching can be continued.

20 Carry on sewing the rolled plait until it is finished at the planned height. Now the plait is finished and the rim is reinforced.

21 Pass the needle between the two groups of strands of the plait and insert the lower group into the basket.

22 Put a stitch in the basket to fix it.

23 Place the other group of strands in an orderly pile and place them next to the last stitch.

24 Fix it to the basket with another stitch below the two strands.

25

26

27

28

25 Now a brightly colored piece is introduced that will complete an entire row at the opening of the basket, to reinforce and embellish it and to lengthen the two groups of strands from the plait.

26 A brightly colored leaf is added to one of the groups inside the basket. It turns towards the outside...
.

27 ...and is stitched to the rim.

28 Some pieces are added to lengthen those that are too short. Add them on both sides, so that the short pieces are covered by the new ones on both sides.

29 Complete a row with this strand and stitch it to the basket.

30 Carry on in the same manner, alternating and adding a colored piece at alternate points (in the inside of the piece), and as many as necessary of the neutral color (between the brightly colored leaf and the basket).

29

30

31 Try to ensure that each stitch covers the rest well; if needed, replace or rearrange them.
Here an entire row has been worked.

31

32 The first piece of the lower strand is finished underneath, pull the needle upwards and then the brightly colored strand is finished.

32

"Try to ensure that each stitch covers the rest well; if needed replace or rearrange them."

33

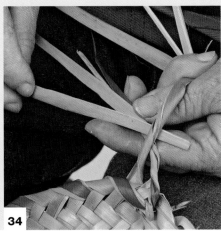

34

33 Now it is time to start the handles. Starting with the two strands that were with the brightly colored piece, make a cord with three pieces per strand.

34 Twist each strand in a clockwise direction and at the same time, pass the right-hand strand over the one on the left, again and again. New pieces can be incorporated as needed between the two strands. Then carry on twisting as before.

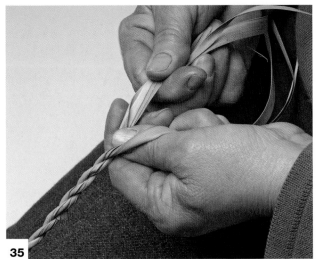

35

35 The strand on the right is twisted and passed over the one on the left.

36 Hold the basket down with your foot to keep the tension in the cord being made.

36

37

*"Starting with the two strands
that were with the brightly colored piece,
make a cord of three pieces per strand."*

38

39

37 For this basket, the cord will need to measure twice the perimeter of the opening of the piece.

38 Try the handle as shown to measure the size that it will have and leave your fingers at the end.

39 Then double the cord over and take two times this measure of cord.

Step by step

40 Hold the cord by this second point, letting the basket hang then turn it so that the cord twists even more.

41 Now hold this section of cord in the middle and see how it twists unaided.

42 Thread the tip of the cord through your needle and pass it all inside the basket.

43 Wrap the cord once more around the handle, positioning it in the grooves left by the previous twisting.

44 With the cord threaded through the needle, fix the handle to the basket.

45 Take the whole cord back outside the piece.

44

45

46 Finish securing the handle with a cross stitch on the outside then cut the leftover cord.

46

47

47 Bring the two sides of the basket together to check where the handle is going to be positioned on the other side.

48 Push the threaded needle outwards from the inside in the chosen place.

49 Fix the start with a pair of cross stitches and repeat the process on the other side.

48

49

The basket combines practical and decorative functions.

A willow
snail cage

This black willow piece is for keeping snails in, although its shape, round and airy, makes it a good multi-purpose container or decorative object. The techniques used are simple and the main difficulty with these rounded shapes is that first they open out, then they close and then they open up again. This piece requires about 100 stems of soaked black willow, of about 150cm so it is best to have at least 130 prepared. Work created by Guillem Manetes.

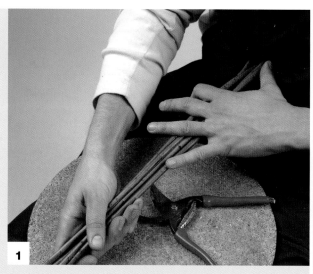

1 Begin with a cross base (see page 32), select nine stems and cut pieces about 25cm long from the thick part.

2 Make a hole in five of the stems with the point of your secateurs and feed the four stems without holes through the five that have them.

3 Prepare two fine weavers to bind the cross. Sharpen the thick end, so that the first centimeters are like split willow. This way, fine willow is being used when you are separating the stems of the cross.

4 Two rows of twining are worked around the center of the cross, with two stems, using the sharpened ends first.

5 On the next row, separate the stems of each arm of the cross into groups of two or three

6 On the next row, separate all the stems in the arms of the cross with an even number of stems into pairs and if the arms have an odd number of stems, separate them into two, one and two stems then separate them into single spokes

7 Continue weaving the base. Now it is woven with two weavers but not with both at the same time: each one moves forwards until it almost reaches the other one, which then starts and moves forward until it almost reaches the first one.

8 When the weave of the diameter reaches 22cm, cut and tuck the ends of the two weavers and cut the protruding stems that are left inside.

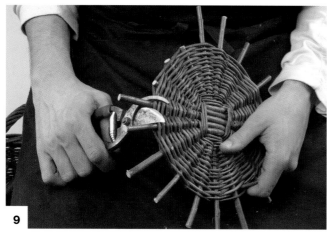

9

10

11

12

9 Also trim the ends of the spokes of the base.

10 Choose and prepare 18 stakes: one for each spoke in the base. Cut a point in them with the secateurs.

11 Insert a stake into the weave at the side of each one of the spokes.

12 Mark the point at which the stakes are to bend with your fingernail and lift them a little to start the angle off.

13 Lift the stakes.

14 Bind them with a strip of rubber (a piece of tire) and a willow pin. This binding will not come undone and is very firm.

13

14

"Lift the stakes and bind them with a strip of rubber."

15

15 Tap the raised stakes until they can go no further into the base and are well positioned.

16 Begin the rim: insert three sharpened weavers into the weave of the base next to three successive stakes and weave the first row with the three together, passing underneath the base. Keep adding weavers so that the rim covers the joins.

16

17 After a second row with three stems, this time placed in the side of the piece, the rim is finished.

18 Select and position 18 weavers, one per stake, and begin to weave the wall in coral weave (see page 49).

19 Once they are in position, the stakes can be untied and are opened forcefully from the base so that the wall begins to open out.

20 Carry on weaving with the stakes wide open.

21

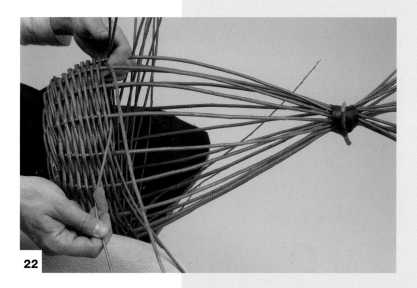
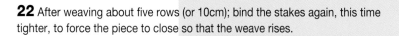

22

21 The piece begins to grow upwards and outwards.

22 After weaving about five rows (or 10cm); bind the stakes again, this time tighter, to force the piece to close so that the weave rises.

23

24

23 When the weavers become too fine, cut them and leave each one behind the nearest stake then replace them.

24 Now position another 18 weavers.

25 Weave this entire group. The diameter now is getting narrower and the rubber binding, which is getting in the way of weaving, can now be removed. Trim the ends when they get too fine, add another group of weavers and continue weaving.

26 Now the opening measures 14cm.

27 The stakes converge and the diameter of the piece is now getting smaller and smaller.

28 Supporting the piece on the floor, force the stakes outwards so that they open out.

29

29 Continue weaving and forcing the new direction. With each step, hold the stake in place ready for the weave to hold it in place.

30 The opening is getting wider. When the desired height is reached, trim all the weavers except two.

31 With these two weavers that are left, weave another row around the opening with the two weavers together to fix the weave.

32 Then start a flat rim, weaving behind one stake and in front of two (see page 51).

30

31

32

"Supporting the piece on the floor, force the stakes towards the outside so that they open out."

33 Here, only the last steps of the flat rim are left to complete.

34 Once the row is finished, the leftover ends are cut beneath the rim.

35 Now position the wrapped stem handle (see page 59). Curve, cut, sharpen and insert both sides of the stem that will be the handle into the weave, next to two stakes separated by another two.

36 Sharpen and insert a stem into the weave at each side to wrap the handle.

"For the cover, make a simple cross base with the last good stems; they should fit in the opening without falling inside the piece."

37 As the handle will be small, you will need to break the stiffness of the stems that are to wrap the handle by twisting from the base to the tip as shown here.

37

38

39

38 Twist the weaver and wrap it three times around the handle, passing it to the other side

39 Pass it under the rim and take it back to the first side, after twisting and wrapping it three times around the handle.

40 Do the same with the weaver from the other side: moving it to one end then back again. As there is still handle to cover; the two weavers make a last journey from one side to the other.

40

41

42

41 Cut and tuck the tips inside the piece and trim them.

42 For the cover make a simple cross base with the last good pieces; it should fit inside the opening without falling inside. Make a small handle.

43 Feed a fine weaver into and out of the top of the cover. Make the handle with the thick, shorter piece by forming a ring with it and attaching it to the other side.

44 Wrap the handle with the thinner, longer part; this little handle can be covered with a couple of wraps. Cut and tuck the ends. With the aid of a pin, this cover will stay on the piece well.

43

44

*Snail cages are an excellent example of the perseverance of
traditional shapes and of how they can be adapted for decorative purposes.*

A willow
and cane basket

This pretty Catalan basket, ancient and modern at the same time, is light, strong and tough. It uses a combination of materials, exploiting the useful properties of each one: cane is a rigid, light material, very prolific in the Mediterranean region; willow is better to work, but it weighs more and it is not as easy to cultivate in places that are prone to droughts.

For this basket you will use 70 stems of 150cm soaked black willow so it is worthwhile preparing at least 90. You will also need 5 newly cut canes and one thicker piece of willow to make the handle. Work by Mònica Guilera.

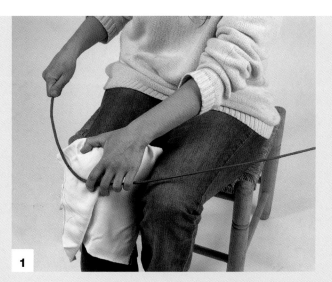

1 To begin the flat base (see page 38 onwards), choose two long stems and start curving them by running them along the front of your knee.

2 First make the hoop with one stem and then reinforce it with another. Try to keep a good balance of thicknesses when you are positioning the stems.

3 Bind the ring to narrow the diameter.

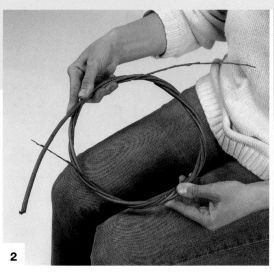

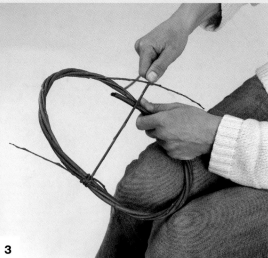

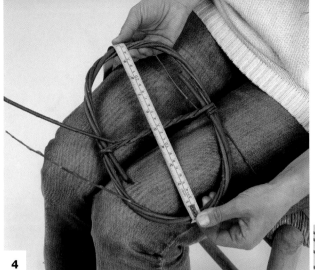

4 Control the size and symmetry of the hoop with a rule. Adjust the binding slightly so that it is positioned right in the middle. This hoop measures 25 x 16cm.

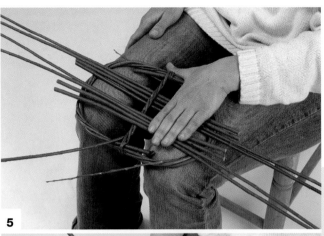

5 With the hoop on your knees, position the stems for the base: place two stems together to each side on top of the hoop and binding, and then another two stems together to each side that pass under the binding but on top of the hoop.
This way, all the stakes needed for the wall of the piece are already in place and no more will need to be added.

6 While holding this still unstable frame with one hand, begin to weave the base at the center.

7 Here four weavers have been woven, two to each side of the binding, alternating directions. These are the stems that will later cover the handles.

8 Carry on weaving. The first three stems are cut short on both sides. The long ends will be used as stakes for the wall, and the short ones will be cut.

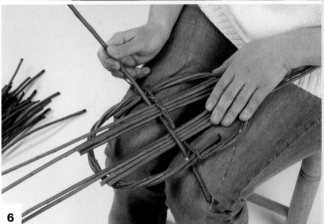

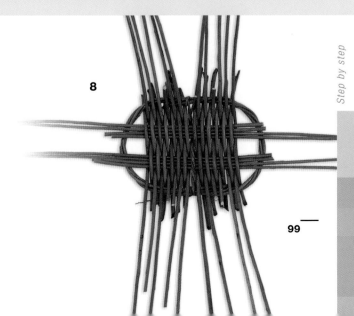

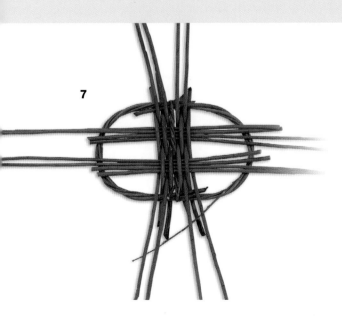

9

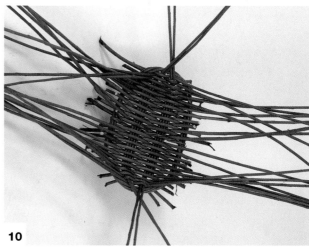

10

11

9 Cut the short ends of the stakes when they are getting close to the hoop, the short ends of the base stakes are cut so that they don't make working the last weavers difficult.

10 The base is very closely woven. Now the ends can be trimmed so that they so not get in the way but they must be left long enough so that they are supported on the hoop.

11 The stakes are raised. Each one has two stems, except those belonging to the handle, which have four. There are two stakes in each point, one (double) on each side of the center and three in each space between point and center. In total there are 18 stakes. Choose the stems that will serve the purpose and raise them and ensure they are well distributed.

12 Bind the raised stems and cut the extra length.

12

13 Begin the rim (see page 47). Sharpen three stems and insert them into the weave at one end and weave the base with three stems together.

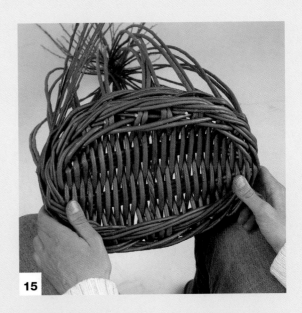

14 Add one weaver to each strand when you begin the second half of the first row.

15 To finish the rim, weave a second row with a three-strand weave of two weavers per strand, but in the side of the piece rather than the base. Then weave a row with a two-strand weave of three weavers per strand, on top of the second row

16 Undo the cage to carry on shaping the piece: separate the stakes at the two ends of the oval, while keeping the central ones closed.

17 Begin to weave the wall with cane that has been split into eight. Take two strips and weave them alternately from left to right, around the stakes so that the lower one is always a little in front of the top one.

18 Each time that a cane finishes or breaks, replace it, with the joins always inside the piece and behind a stake. The weave always uses two pieces of cane at a time.

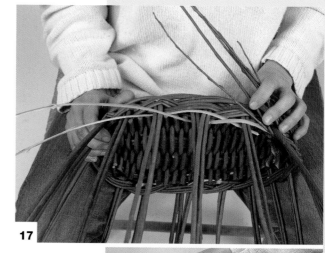

17

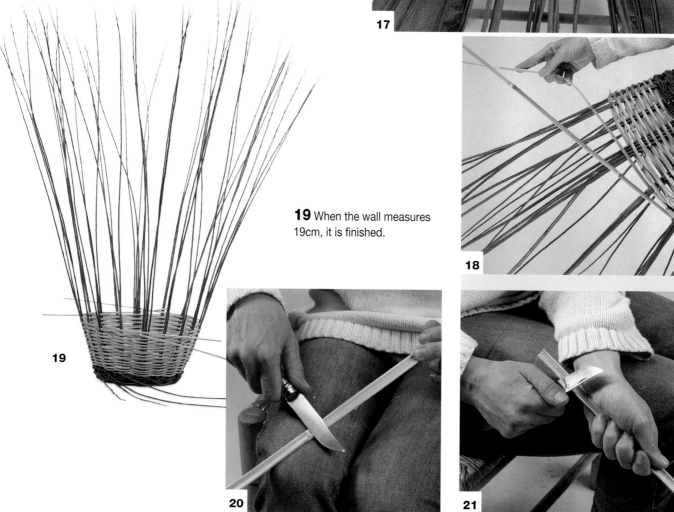

18

19 When the wall measures 19cm, it is finished.

19

20

21

20 Now it is time to insert pieces of cane, that has been split into four (the ribs), into the weave at the side of the stakes. This tensions the warp and gives stiffness to the piece. Scrape the cane to get rid of any bits sticking out from the nodes.

21 There will be twice as many ribs as stakes: 36. Make a point at the thinnest end of a cane.

22 Insert the sharpened end of the cane into the base, if possible as far as the rim.

23 At the side of the stake, the ends of the two canes are left facing each other. Cut the canes so that they are flush with the border if they have been inserted from the base and leave them a little longer if they have been inserted further up.

24 Tap the canes that haven't gone in far enough until they are inserted into the rim. Once all the stakes have two cane ribs, the wall is finished.

"Once all the stakes have two cane ribs, the wall is finished."

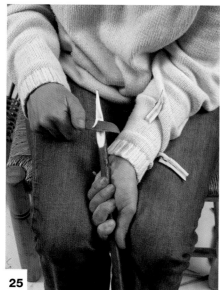

25

25 Next, prepare the handle. To do this this, take a thicker stem cut to measure (the part of the handle that can be seen plus the height of the two walls) and sharpen points on the two sides so that it can be inserted it into the weave.

26 Curve the center piece of the handle without marking an angle. Smear the ends with beeswax (paraffin or animal fat will do as well) to make them slide better and easier to insert.

"There are two stakes in every end, one (double) at each side of the center and three in each space between end and center. In total, 18 stakes."

26

27 Find the place where the handle will be attached, which must be nice and central. Open up a gap with a bodkin, helping with your legs, and fix the handle securely on both sides. Check the shape of the piece and make adjustments if the piece is no longer symmetrical.

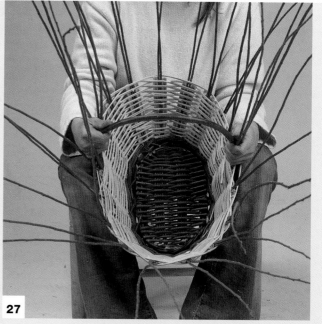

27

28 Begin the rope trim (see page 55, although this handle is different and the start of the rim is different too). At the second stake before the handle add two stems and at the first stake add one stem.

29 Position a small rod next to the fourth stake before the handle to simulate the thickness of the strand that will finish the row. Lower the two stems of the stake together, twist them and pass them in front of the next stake and between the stems of the double stake towards the center.

30 The finish is complete. Leave the handle and the four stems of its stakes standing on the two sides. Pass two strands of the rim outwards and one strand to the inside of the piece.

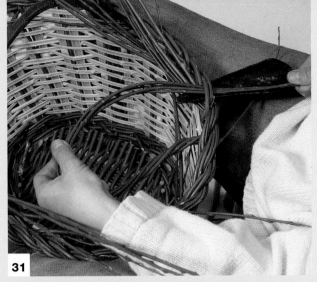

31 Open a gap so that the last strands of the rope trim can pass through to finish.

32 Trim the ends left inside the piece.

33 Now the handle is being wrapped (see page 59) with the four stems that were left upright on each side. Begin with those from one side; wrap them around the handle three times. Then do the same with the ones from the other side.

34 Cut and tuck the ends of the stems that wrapped the handle between the strands of the rope and finish trimming the piece.

View of the finished basket where the interesting contrast between the materials can be appreciated.

Coiled bread
basket

Using only basic techniques and adaptations of these, this basket maker has invented and created a piece with a fun contrast between different willows, and which plays with two coils: one that shows off the depth of the colors and one that provides the structure of the piece. Use 140cm-long stems of two different colored varieties of soaked black willow, and a thicker rod for the mast. Work by Joan Farré.

1 Begin with a four-by-four cross base (see page 32): cut eight stems of about 25cm, which will be the spokes of the base.

2 Open up a gap in one of them by inserting the point of the knife and twisting to separate the grain of the wood.

3 Insert a stake in the open gap.

4

4 Next, repeat the process with the others until you have a cross of four-by-four stems.

5 With two stems, starting at the thick end, make two rows of twining with two stems at a time around all four arms (see page 34).

5

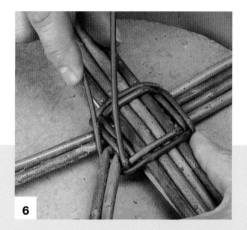

6

7

6 On the next row separate them into pairs.

7 Still twining with two weavers at a time, separate all the stakes into single spokes.

8 Now, to achieve the coil effect in the base, weave the rest of the base using coral weave (see page 49) and introduce a contrasting color. Position 16 weavers starting at their thin ends.

8

9

10

9 All the weavers in position are green, except a row of six, which are brown.

10 Complete another row with each weaver, but without allowing the ones on the left to overtake the ones on the right.

11 The brown weavers mark out a spiral on the base that begins at the thin end and increases in thickness. Carry on weaving the base until it reaches about 20cm in diameter.

12 Trim the ends and leave one tucked under each stake. Do not trim them too drastically, just enough so that they are not in the way. Now attach two weavers in two consecutive spokes for finishing the base.

11

12

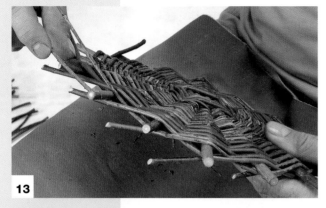

13

"The brown weavers mark out a spiral on the base that begins at the thin end and increases in thickness."

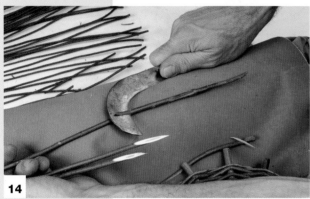

14

13 Next, the base is finished with a row of two weavers.

14 Choose the stems to be inserted next to the spokes (27 in total) and cut a point at one end of each.

15 Insert them into the weave: two per spoke – one on each side. Insert another two by the next spoke then one by the following spoke.

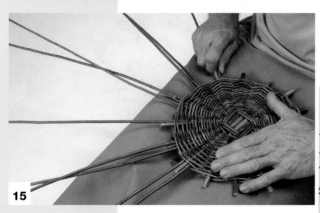

15

16 Repeat this pattern (two, two, and one) four more times. There will be one spoke left over in the base, insert a stem at each side of this. At this point, the 27 stakes have been positioned.

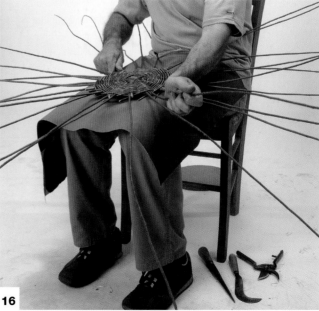

16

17 Begin to raise the stakes to make the cage. Work with precision.

18 Use a nail to mark the angle.

19 Tie the cage with a weaver.

"The rim has three rows woven with three weavers, although each trio of weavers has only completed one and a half rows."

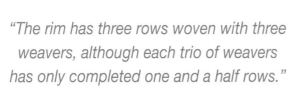

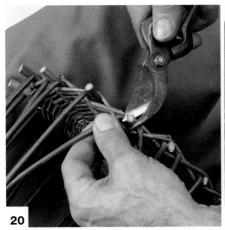

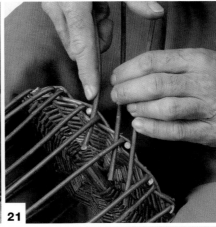

20

21

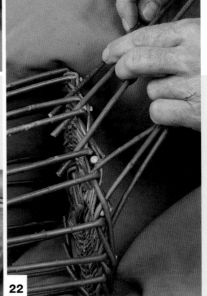

22

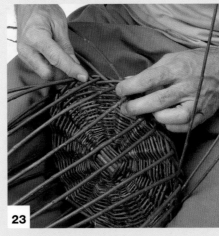

23

20 Once the stakes are attached, cut the ends of the spokes, keeping the new stems out of the way so they do not get damaged.

21 Now insert the first three weavers for the rim and begin a row with all three of them.

22 Turn the piece around and position three stems in the opposite side, in front of the first ones, to continue the rim.

24

23 Each trio advances in turn, moving three weavers at a time but the trio on the left never overtakes the one on the right.

24 Three rows of the rim have been completed with three weavers being moved at a time although each trio of weavers has only completed one and a half rows.

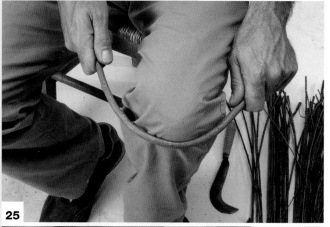

25

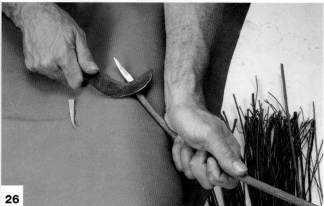

26

25 Take a stake of about two handspans in length; it should be thicker than the spokes in the base. Bend it by running it along the front of your knee. This will be the mast.

26 Sharpen the mast at one end.

27 Insert it into the weave of the rim, next to a stake.

28 Cut the binding of the cage.

27

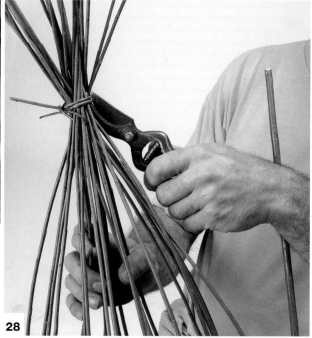

28

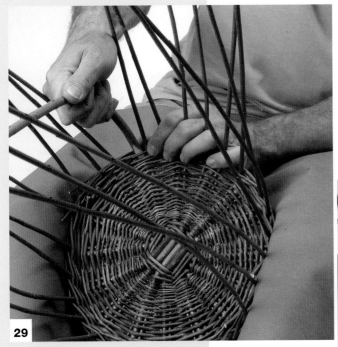

29

"This piece uses a coral weave but using one weaver at a time with alterations because the piece is not circular, and also to obtain the desired different levels."

30

31

29 Decide the curve of the center stake. This piece uses a coral weave (see page 49), but using one weaver at a time with alterations because the piece is not circular, and also to obtain the desired different levels.

30 Begin with a weaver behind the second stake before the mast. It moves forward, and then when it reaches the mast it turns and goes back, repeats the process once and is cut behind the stake.

31 Start another weaver at the next stake on the left, this one also weaves towards the mast and then back again. Each new weaver begins at the stake to the left of the previous one, goes forward to the mast and then back. When positioning the weavers, alternate the thin and thick ends to balance thicknesses.

32 Whenever it seems necessary (now, for example), wind the weaver that is in play once around the mast.

32

Step by step

33

34

33 From time to time, instead of stopping after going back after the mast, weave forwards again. The purpose of this is to add height to the right hand side close to the mast.

34 Remember to keep shaping to the mast, since otherwise it tends to become straight. You will also need to force the weave towards the inside at a determined height.

35

36

35 and **36** Once the warp has been inserted by all the positioned stakes, a second row is added in front of the one already woven, inserting seven new stakes into the weave of the rim with the help of a bodkin.

37

38

39

40

41

37 The new stakes have been inserted. They are somewhat finer than the others so that they can adapt to the shape of the piece.

38 and **39** Continue the weave, now around the new stakes, from the base to the mast.

40 Carry on weaving backwards and forwards close to the mast to add height on the right hand side.

41 The last weaver is inserted into the inner layer.

42 The weave is finished: it begins flush with the border on the left and rises abruptly when it gets close to the center stake.

43 Check and correct the shape, pressing the weave...

"Start the flat rim, behind two and in front of three."

44 Fix the end of the weave with a row of a group of three weavers (see page 46), inserting three weavers to the side of the first three stakes.

45 Complete the end of the row by twisting the third weaver around the mast.

46 Start the flat rim (see page 51), behind two and in front of three. Since it is not a round piece, you will need to attach four weavers, which will be the first four weavers to be bent down.

47 and **48** These new weavers must be positioned next to each other as if they had already passed behind two and are now passing in front of three (only from the point into which they are inserted).

46

47

48

49 The first stake is bent down and passes behind two next to one of the newly added stakes.

49

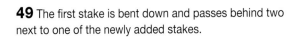

50

50 Continue with the rim: first behind two stakes (first stage) and then in front of three (second and last stage) to leave after the next one, which is next to the other that is bent down and passed behind two.

51 The rim moves forwards and gets closer to the mast.

52 and **53** Now it is time to cut and tuck the rim: the first weaver of the fourth pair passes around the mast and comes back to the right where it came from.

54 The first weaver of the next pair does the same.

55 All the protruding ends are trimmed. The mast and the upright stakes are cut diagonally following the dynamic of the piece.

Viewed from a new perspective, the use of basic techniques allows us to create innovative solutions.

A chestnut strip
"desca"

"Desca" is the Catalan name for a traditional Pyrenean piece made from strips of wood, with a structure of ribs and handles at the ends; it has a simple elegance and stands up to every test. Roger Chinaud made this one with chestnut in the green, which means that it has been recently cut or cut up to a week ago; that way it is whiter than if it had been soaked. About five rods of chestnut are used for a piece like this; these can be chosen and prepared during the weaving process as needed.

1 and **2** Look for and select the material. Three-year-old shoots from a coppiced tree have been chosen here. They have no branches, are between two fingers and one handspan thick and have an olive green color.

3 and **4** Here the shoots are being cut with a saw and the excess pieces are discarded. Selective work helps to keep the chestnut tree in good condition.

5

6

7

5 To measure for the handle, a previously made desca is being turned on one of the rods, from one handle to the other, and then cut.

6 At 10cm from each end make a crosswise incision with a saw.

7 and **8** Starting from one incision, split the rod as far as the other incision, separating the grain, first with an axe and then with the hands.

8

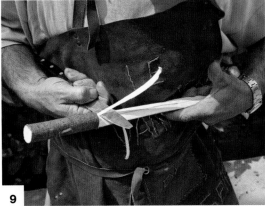

9 and **10** With a knife level the open part and smooth the ends.

11 Curve the handle.

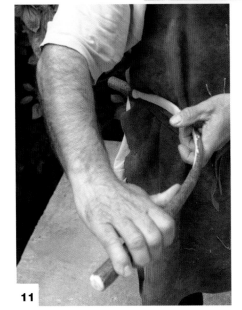

12 and **13** Hammer a nail into each end and attach a cord that will hold the arched shape during work.

"Prepare several strips for weaving: take a quarter of a rod, remove the heart and the rest can be split into very fine strips."

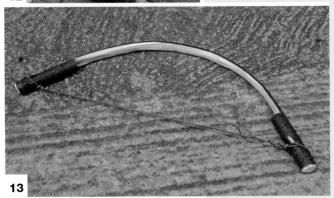

14

15

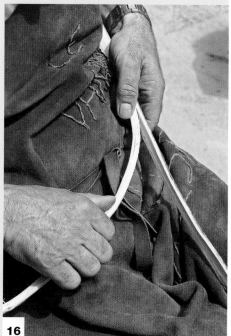

16

14 and **15** Prepare the first strip, which will be the hoop. Split a rod into four lengthwise by first splitting it in half then splitting each half in two. Now peel the bark off; an easy task in the summer.

16 The heart has a triangular cross section, remove this. This will leave a strip with a rounded shape on the outside.

17 and **18** Bend this strip into a circular shape and fit this hoop into the cleft part of the handle.

17

18

19

20

19 and **20** Shape the ends of the strip so that they couple together then close the hoop, nailing it in place. Also nail the hoop to the handle at the joined part.

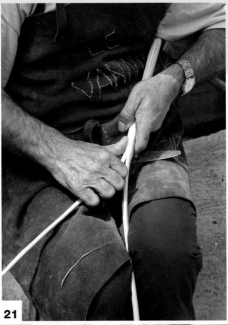

21

22

23

21 Prepare several strips for weaving: take a quarter of a rod, remove the heart and the rest can be split into very fine strips.

22 and **23** Carry on separating about four strips per side. A strip corresponds to one year's growth of the tree.

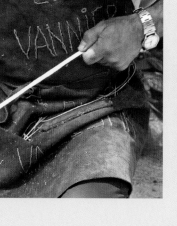

24

25

24 Smooth, sharpen and make the strips equal by sliding them along between the knee and the knife.

25 With one of the strips, bind the central point and the hoop together with a cross.

26 After the cross, weave (behind, in front, behind, in front...) from one side to the other of the hoop. If a strip finishes, bring in a new one a couple of steps before it ends.

27 and **28** When this binding is finished tie the end and repeat the process on the other side.

26

27

"If a strip finishes, bring in a new one a pair of steps before it ends."

28

29

30

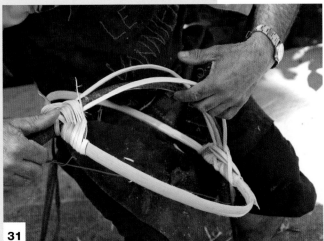

31

"Try to maintain this relation of lengths to make a double cavity and for better stability for the piece."

29 Take a strip with a triangular cross section, from one of the hearts removed from the rod, to make the first rib. Take the measurement over the handle and cut it to size.

30 Insert this rib into one of the cross ties, curve it over and insert the other end in the other cross, beside the handle.

31 Place another rib in the other side, keeping the symmetry of the piece; for this, measure, cut, sharpen, attach, curve and finally attach to the other side.

32 The next pair will be the closest to the hoop.

32

33

33 and **34** Position another pair beside the first. To introduce the ends into the cross it is best to sharpen them first.

35 It is good to maintain this set of lengths to create a double cavity and for greater stability for the piece.

36 The last pair of ribs is in position: there are four ribs at each side.

34

35

36

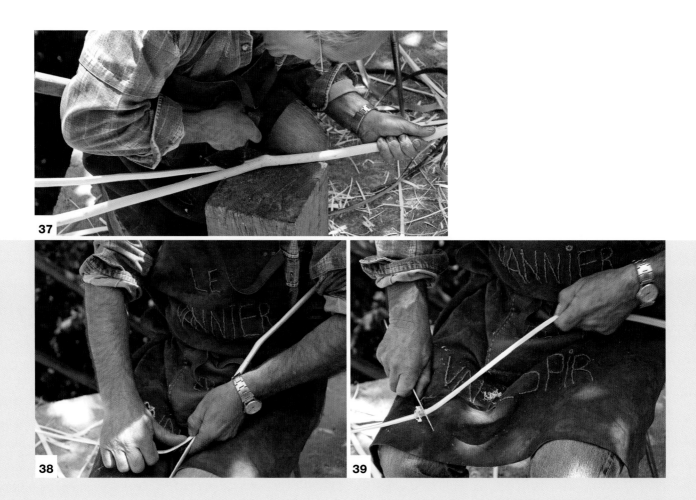

37, 38 and 39 Carry on preparing more strips of the sizes needed. Split the rods from top to bottom with the axe, varying the angle to control the direction of the split; remove the heart; and from the rest take three fine strips and smooth them with the knife.

40 and 41 When preparing the strips, some difficulties may arise, for example, when the wood is damaged, or there is a knot in the wood. The solution is to cut off the defective part.

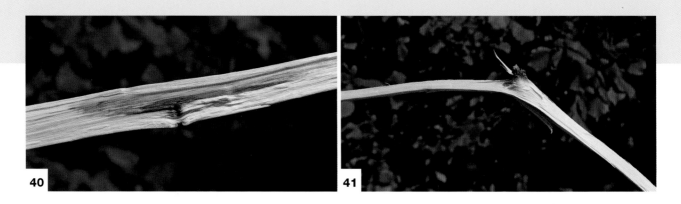

42 Now the frame is made, and weaving can begin. To start with weave two under, two over.

42

43

43 Continue this pattern, forwards and backwards. The handle counts as another rib and is wrapped once around the hoop.

44 and **45** Now weave them one by one.

44

45

"The weave advances from the two sides towards the center by alternating weaving one strip on each side."

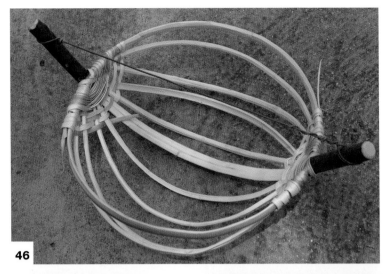

46 The weave advances from the two sides towards the center by alternating weaving one strip on each side

47 and **48** When the second strip is woven, split it in two to cross the handle to narrow it, and then work the two halves together after crossing the handle.

49 The strip is wound once around the hoop.

"By sharpening the strips in the center, space can be gained in the hoop so that the two sides come closer in parallel."

50

51

50 The two sides should look like two parallel lines that are getting closer rather than two semicircles. To do this split each strip in two to work the central part.

51 When a strip is ending, work another one in next to it for two steps before it ends.

52 and **53** Regularly press and adjust the weave, controlling the shape... From time to time, weave with a thicker strip to add strength to the piece.

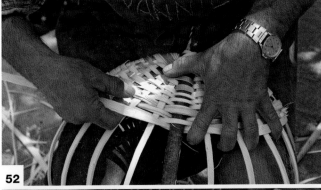

52

53

54 By sharpening the strips in the center, space can be gained in the hoop so that the two sides come closer in parallel.

55, 56 and **57** So that the weave does not become loose, wait until the next day to weave the last strips as the wood shrinks somewhat as it dries. The cord can be cut when the piece is dry.

*"So that the weave does not become loose, wait until
the next day to weave the last strips as the wood shrinks
somewhat as it dries."*

Several finished descas. They are strong pieces good
for carrying heavy loads.

Gallery

Julie Gurr, Limpet Basket, 2004.
Willow with limpet shells (17 x 23 cm).
Photograph by Shannon Tofts.

Manuel Sancho, Mannequin, 2002.
Rattan medulla (43 x 21 x 16 cm).

Joanna Gilmour, Darwin's Baskets, 2003. Paper cords, diagonal
weave tube, knotted coil, glass tank (77 x 30 x 30 cm).
Photograph by Steven Hicks.

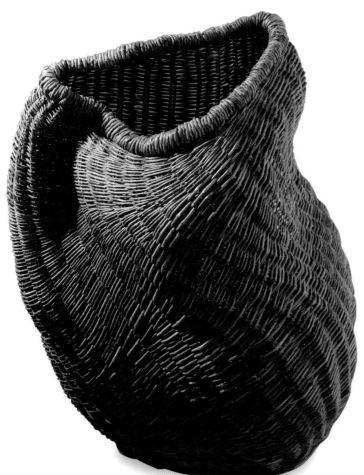

Lizzie Farey, Pussy willow bowl, 2004.
Flowering willow (50 cm diameter).
Photograph by Shannon Tofts.

Klaus Seyfang, Basket, 2002.
Willow (100 x 60 cm).
Photograph by Joachim Rommel, Bild-Media.

Gallery

Christine Adcock, Jacaranda Basket, 2006.
Spherical basket made with dyed palm
flowers and jacaranda seed pods
(35.56 x 25.4 cm).
Photograph by Mehosh Dziadzio.

Manuel Sancho, Chess board and pieces,
1999. Rattan medulla (board: 45 3 45 cm,
pieces: 15 cm high).

Alison Fitzgerald, Aplique, 2005.
Willow (60 x 50 cm).

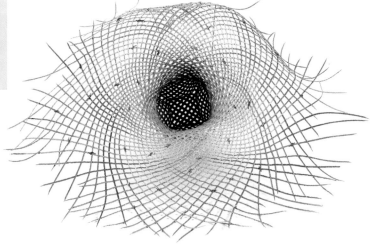

Caroline Gregson, Sedimentation, 2005.
Various varieties of willow, anodized
aluminium and steel (each panel: 14 x 33 cm).

Joanna Gilmour, Flycatcher, 2002. Paper cords, plaited and
knotted (70 x 28 cm). Photograph by Steven Hicks.

Pont de Querós,
Linoculus, 2006.
Living willow.
Photograph by
Carme Sitjà.

Gallery

Dieter Deringer, Cradle, 2005. Ergonomic hanging rocking cradle made with white and buff willow. (105 x 55 x 50 cm).

Palma, 2006. Traditional piece made with date palm for Palm Sunday.

Joan Farré, Baskets, 2006. Willow and cane. Traditional Catalan basketry pieces. Photograph by Carme Sitjà.

Josep Mercader, En dansa, 2006. Installation from the series, Variable Geometries. Black willlow. Made for the expedition Temps de Flors 13th to 21st May 2006, Girona.

Alison Fitzgerald, Sciathog, 2004.
Willow and hazel (45 cm diameter).

Blind, 2006. Traditional roller blind from the southern Iberian peninsula made with plaited esparto and reinforced stitching.

A – Awl. Tool used to open a space in the weave so that another stem or strip can be passed through it.

B- Bamboo. Similar to cane, this material has a long tradition of use in oriental basketry.

Base. The bottom of the basket. In many cases it is fundamental to the structure of the piece.

Basket. Concave, rigid piece designed to hold items.

Bread basket. Concave piece without handles used to contain bread and other products.

C – Cane (*Arundo donax*). Fairly rigid material that is usually worked after splitting.

Chestnut (*Castanea sativa*). Rigid material, usually worked in strips.

Cleave. To split a wooden rod, a cane, etc., lengthwise into two or more strips of the same length, separating the grain of the plant without cutting. Also the name of the tool used for the task. Used especially with cane and willow.

Coil. Ancient and very widespread basketry structure shaped like a snail shell and usually worked with soft materials.

Coral weave. A weave made with an equal number of weavers and stakes.

Cross base. A base constructed and woven on a frame of crossed strips or stems.

Cut and tuck. Finish a weave by folding the stems that are left on the outside of the basket to the inside so that they do not come undone.

D – Desca. A traditional Pyrenean piece made with wooden strips, a hoop, a central rod and rib structure.

E – Esparto (*Stipa tenecissima*). Material typical of countries with hot dry climates. It is thin, flexible and strong.

Espuerta. Concave piece with two small handles on the sides, made with flexible materials.

F – Flat base. Base constructed on a hoop and two parallel stakes.

H – Hazel (*Corylus avellana*). Woody material worked in rods or strips.

P – Palm. Basketry material obtained from palm leaves.
Plait. Long narrow strip of flexible material with diagonal weave used for various pieces.

R – Rattan (*Calamus rotang* and other species). Material in long, even, flat strips or in circular sections (medulla).
Reed. This material can be obtained from several plants from humid areas and has various applications in basketry.
Rib. Part of the structure of some pieces, especially those made from woody materials.
Rim. Part of the weave of a piece than joins the base to the walls. Also refers to the top of the weave of the basket walls.
Rod. Long, straight, thin branch.
Rush (*Typha latifolia* and *Typha angustifolia*). Soft flexible material, often used in basketry.

S – Snail cage (*caracolera*). Covered piece designed to keep snails in before cooking them.
Soak. Impregnate the dried material with water so that it gains flexibility when ready to be worked.
Spoke. The spokes are the weft of some types of bases, such as the round base.
Stake. Fundamental part of the structure of many pieces, serving as the weft for the weave.
Straw. This material can be obtained from many different plant species, mostly from cereals.
Strip. Material in strip form, like tape, usually prepared by splitting wooden rods or cane.

W – Warp. The weave that is made on the weft, more or less perpendicular to it and interlaced with it.
Weft. Structure made from parallel pieces on which the warp is made.
Willow (*Salix viminalis* and other species). Woody material usually worked in rods although also split into strips. This material is very flexible when wet but rigid when dry.

Bibliography

• Barbier, G. y Pichonnet, M.
La vannerie: rotin et osier.
Dessain et Tolra, 2003.

• Butcher, M. *Contemporary International Basketmaking.* Merrell Holberton & Crafts Council, London, 1999.

• Duchesne, R., Ferrand, H. & Thomas, J. *La vannerie, l'osier.* Dominique Guéniot et École Nationale d'Osiériculture et de Vannerie, Langres, 1997.

• Fontales, C. *Cestería de los pueblos de Galicia,* IR Indo Edicións, Vigo, 2006.

• Gabriel, S. y Goymer, S. *The Complete Book of Basketry Techniques.* David & Charles, London, 1999.

• Hogan, J. *Basketmaking in Ireland.* Wordwell, 2001.

• Kuoni, B. *Cestería tradicional ibérica.* El Serbal, Barcelona, 2003.

• Vaughan, S. *Handmade Baskets: From Nature's Colorful Material.* Search Press, Londres, 1994.

• Wright, D. *Complete Book of Basketry.* Dover Publications, Mineola, New York, 2001.

Acknowledgments

To the Associació Catalana de Cistellers and all their members for their generosity and warmth; especially Roser Albó, Carles Alcoy, Joan Farré, Mònica Guilera, Josep Mercader, Guillem Manetes, Carlus Trijueque, Raquel Serres, Rosario Vidiella, Manolo Sancho, Roger Chinaud and Lluís Grau, who have taught and helped us and encouraged us with their enthusiasm as well as lending us pieces, tools and materials whenever we have needed them. To Pilar Álvarez Pablos for her help with dying the willow, to Teresa Lladó for allowing the photo sessions to take place at her house, to Joana Barber for her help with the location of the photographs. To Ana Ullibarri and to the Romanís for lending us some of the pieces included in this book.

To the artists:

Christine Adcock
www.adcockstudios.com

Roger Chinaud
Moulin de la Palette. 66110 Amélie les Bains

Flechtwerk. Dieter Deringer
www.flechtwerk-dieter-deringer.de

Lizzie Farey
www.lizziefarey.co.uk

Joan Farré Oliver
Jfarre01@terra.es

Alison Fitzgerald
alison@greenwoodbaskets.com

Mònica Guilera
mguilera@tiscali.es

Joanna Gilmour
joannagilmour@phonecoop.coop

Caroline Gregson
www.carolinegregson.com

Julie Gurr
www.willowweaver.com

Felicity Irons. Rush Matters
www.rushmatters.co.uk

Guillem Manetes
mguilera@tiscali.es

Josep Mercader
josepnic03@yahoo.com

Pont de Querós. Dinàmiques amb Vímet
pontdequeros@terra.es

Manolo Sancho
msancho@fincassanchogil.com

Klaus Seyfang
www.geflecht-klaus.de

Raquel Serres
margallopinell@hotmail.com

project and production:
Parramón ediciones, S.A.

chief editor:
Ma Fernanda Canal

assistant editor and image archive
Ma Carmen Ramos

coordination and texts
Caterina Hernàndez and Eva Pascual

exercise production
Caterina Hernàndez, Roger Chinaud, Joan Farré, Mònica Guilera, Guillem Manetes, Raquel Serres and Rosario Vidiella

collection design
Josep Guasch

layout and page make up
Estudi Guasch, S.L.

photographs
Nos & Soto

head of production
Rafael Marfil

production
Manel Sánchez

prepress
Pacmer, S.A.

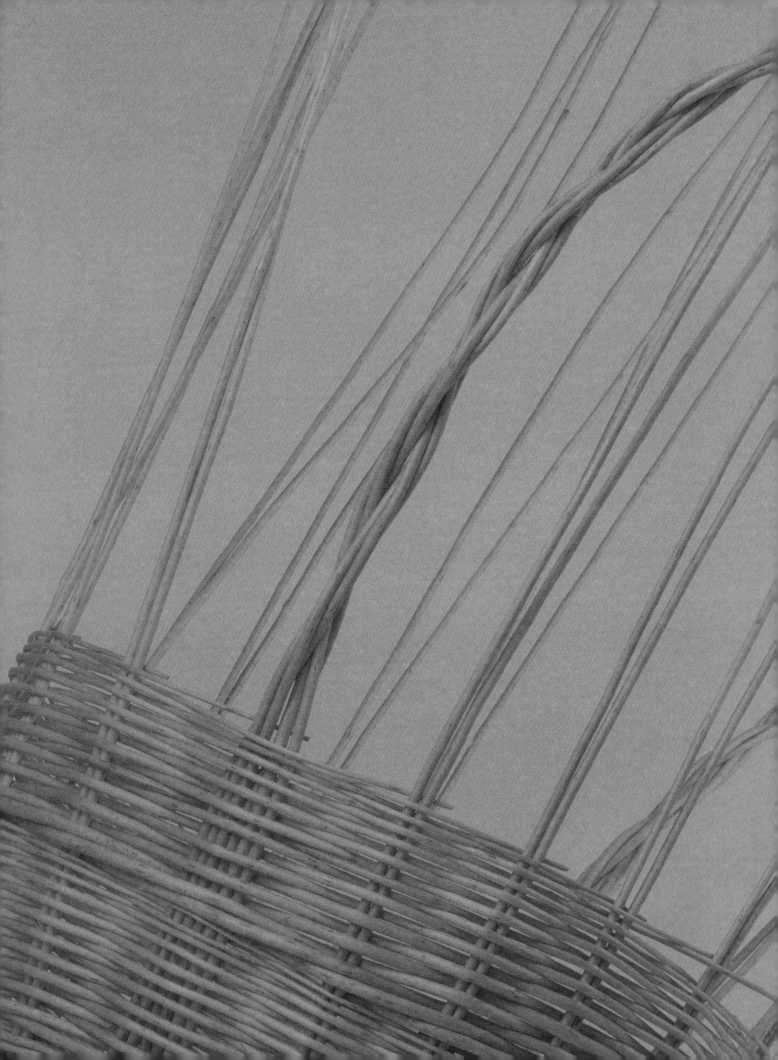